Falcon™ Air Combat

Pete Bonanni

**Silicon
Valley**

Osborne **McGraw-Hill**
2600 Tenth Street
Berkeley, California 94710
U.S.A.

For information on translations and book distributors outside of the
U.S.A., please write to Osborne **McGraw-Hill** at the above address.

A complete list of trademarks appears on page 193.

Falcon™ Air Combat

1234567890 DOC 89

ISBN 0-07-881543-6

Acquisitions Editor: Stephen Hom
Associate Editor: Roger Stewart
Project Editor: Nancy Beckus
Technical Reviewer: Robert Bonanni
Copy Editor: Ann Kraeger Spivak
Proofreaders: Barbara Conway, Julie Anjos
Word Processor: Judy Koplan
Composition: Bonnie Bozorg
Technical Illustration: Peter Hancik
Book Design: Judy Wohlfrom
Production Supervisor: Kevin Shafer

This book was produced using Ventura Publisher Version 2. Cover art by Steven
Black Design, Inc. F-16 photo courtesy of General Dynamics. Color separation by
Colour Image. Cover supplier, Phoenix Color Corp. Screens produced with Inset
from Inset Systems, Inc.

Contents

Acknowledgments

This book is the result of a team effort. I would like to thank my brother Bob Bonanni for doing the screen shots and technical editing, and many other essential tasks. Credit also goes to Steve Hom of Osborne/McGraw-Hill for his many contributions as editor. I would also like to thank my uncle, Dominick Castelli, and my aunt, Kathryn MacKnight Castelli, for their crucial and timely help, which made this book possible.

Most important, I thank my wife, Teresa, who provided the inspiration for this project.

Introduction

The realism that makes Falcon such a good computer game can unfortunately leave the simulator pilot bewildered as he faces an intimidating combat flight environment with very little training or preparation. If you feel like a "hood ornament on a beam of light" every time you try to poke your nose into the "Falcon World," this book is for you. *Falcon Air Combat* will provide you direction and purpose to help you control the jet and the tactical environment.

This book was written from a fighter pilot's perspective and, as such, is littered with fighter pilot terms and jargon. I've tried to define most of these terms in text. Despite the jargon, the book provides straightforward instruction that centers around accomplishing tactical objectives with skill and style. There are several flying stories and examples in the book which will hopefully help readers project into the game and build their own tactical perspectives of air combat. The most important part of the book is the step-by-step instruction, which ensures that the Falcon pilot can fight and win the air battle.

Material for this book was gathered by flying the simulation using a Macintosh, an IBM XT, and an IBM AT. The screen shots and the instructions referencing specific computer keys were taken from the IBM AT computer.

Well enough of an introduction—it is time to learn the art of Falcon Air Combat. Read on.

The Game of Falcon

Few could argue with Falcon's appeal, much of which comes from the uncompromising realism that its creator, Gilman Louie, insisted upon when his team originally wrote the program. But if you have played Falcon extensively, you no doubt realize that it is a game that seems to get better as player proficiency increases. Certainly, fast reflexes and intimate familiarity with the myriad of enabling keystrokes go a long way toward winning in Falcon. But to gain real proficiency and consistency, one needs to *think like a fighter pilot,* and therein lies Falcon's real appeal.

Falcon is an intellectual's game and so is today's aerial combat. Unlike earlier jets such as the F-100 and F-4, fighters such as the F-16 with its fly-by-wire flight control system are easy to fly. Flying the jet is not the problem. The hardest task the fighter pilot faces is that of collecting, interpreting, and acting on information derived from his suite of cockpit avionics. The ability to process that information, and to consider dozens of external factors such as flight management, communication jamming, radar sorting, targeting, shot selection, self-defense measures, and so on, is what fighter pilots call *situational awareness.* SA means staying on top of a situation, planning and adjusting in response to the fluid and rapidly changing air- to-air environment. It is, more than any other factor, the key to success in today's aerial combat arena.

Falcon is not a game about flying jets. It is a game of situational awareness, which depends on a firm understanding and appreciation of those basic fighter axioms that have been learned the hard way since men began to fight with airplanes. Captain Pete Bonanni has written this book to provide that basic understanding of the history and fundamental tactics of fighter employment, and to draw appropriate parallels with the scenarios and mission within Falcon.

Having known Pete Bonanni both professionally and socially for several years, I can attest that he is equal to the task. He is a second-generation fighter pilot who grew up in an Air Force family. Pete attended the USAF Academy and has flown the F-4, A-7, and F-16. In this book, I think he has achieved a near perfect blend of history, tactics, and technique, and accented them with personal experience and anecdotes directly related to appropriate scenarios in Falcon.

So, what's the big deal about a computer game? If you have already played Falcon, you understand my enthusiasm. If you haven't, you've got a real treat ahead of you. When I first slipped Falcon into my Macintosh Plus about two years ago, I was skeptical. Although, I didn't bother to give Falcon's accompanying manual more than a cursory glance before booting up and taking off, I was impressed by the fact that the manual was organized along the lines of a typical Air Force Dash-1, which I thought was a nice touch. However, I also noted that the user's proficiency level was equated to military rank. Coupling proficiency with rank is fine, but as a retired Air Force officer who flew F-86s through F-15s at ranks ranging from second lieutenant through full colonel, I can assure you that assigning top proficiency to the rank of colonel is severely flawed.

After selecting the "Lieutenant Level" and taking off, I realized that the aero model driving Falcon was overpowered. I could go straight up, straight down, bounce off the ground, and zap the dreaded MiG-21 at will with missiles that never missed. However, switching to the "Colonel Level" immediately served me up a large dish of "humble pie" as I repeatedly died enroute to the target while I struggled to manipulate the keyboard. I was heartened by the fact that all my instincts appeared to be correct—that the experience I had gained over many years of flying fighters seemed to directly apply to Falcon. The longer I played Falcon, the better and more challenging it became. It was obvious that a great deal of thoughtful attention to detail had gone into its creation. Apparently its author had banked on the hunch that presenting an unembellished scenario of aerial combat would be exciting enough on its own merit.

I was pleased when the opportunity arose for me to meet the author. His name is Gilman Louie. The first time I saw him he was sitting at the keyboard of an IBM AT playing Falcon. If real fighters were flown with keyboards, this guy would be an ace before anyone else got off the runway. The thousands of hours he has spent with Falcon had given his fingers perfect dexterity and keyboard memory. Even more impressive was the fact that this guy, who had never flown in a fighter in his life, employed the F-16 in a very tactically sound manner. He kept his energy high, constantly checked his deep six, jinked coming off the target, flew good basic fighter maneuvers at the merge, defeated missiles with flares and chaff, launched weapons within parameters, and did a hundred other subtle things that I would have never expected a novice to do. I wondered how he did it. After talking with him a few hours, I knew.

There's an old saying in Air Force circles that: "Fighter pilot is an attitude, not an AFSC (Air Force Specialty Code)." Had Gilman Louie been blessed with the 20/20 vision required for admission into flight training, I have no doubt that he would be strapping himself into a first-class fighter today instead of writing software. It is our good fortune that Gilman wasn't qualified to fly; otherwise, we would not have gotten the chance to experience the thrill of simulated flight through Falcon.

Pete Bonanni's book will enable you to experience this thrill. I recommend it to all those who would like to learn the basics of the game quickly, and then use Bonanni's strategies to get as much enjoyment as possible from playing Falcon. Written by a quality fighter pilot, it is a very readable and credible piece of work. Good hunting and check six.

Phil "Hands" Handley
Colonel, USAF (Retired)

Command Pilot with 7,000 flying hours
Two combat tours in Southeast Asia (325 combat sorties)
Flew F-4D & F-4E in combat
MiG killer
21 Air Medals, 3 Distinguished Flying Crosses, 1 Silver Star
Commanded 405th Tactical Training Wing (F-15 & F-5) at Luke AFB, AZ
Retired 1984
Currently: Aviation Simulation Systems Manager, Perceptronics, Inc.

TO FLY
AND FIGHT

1

"To be a successful soldier, you must know history."

—General George S. Patton

You were at the squadron at 0430 planning this mission with a stomach full of butterflies, wishing you'd had more sleep and less whiskey the night before. You've just completed your final preflight checklist; your Falcon is number one for the active runway. All your life you have waited for this moment but now that it's here you wonder if you're really ready.

As you wait to take off the words of the intelligence officer run through your mind: "A Soviet combined arms division has broken through the lines in the U.S. Fifth Corps area, and elements of the Eighth Infantry Division are moving up to stop the breakthrough. The Tenth Tactical Fighter Squadron is flying ground attack missions into the area to slow the advancing Soviet troops. Our Squadron will be flying a MiG sweep mission to support the Tenth. You should not have trouble locating the enemy. The last flight from the area reported MiGs directly over the battle zone. Your thoughts are interrupted as the tower clears you to go.

You taxi your Falcon out onto the runway and line up for take off. As you step down hard on the brakes and run the power up to check the engine, a wave of confidence sweeps over you. The Falcon shudders as the brakes strain to hold it in place. When you finally release the brakes and push the power up to afterburner, you're pressed back in the seat as the Falcon quickly accelerates past 100 knots. At 150 knots you rotate the nose up ten degrees, and the jet springs from the ground. You grab the gear handle and flip it up as the Falcon passes 180 knots. You are airborne and riding on 25,000 lbs of thrust. The ground rushes by as you pass 400 knots and level off. Turning toward the battle zone you think out loud, "someone's going to the meat locker before this fight is over, and it ain't going to be me."

You have just entered the fast-paced, lethal world of the Falcon fighter pilot, where your jet, mother nature, and the enemy all conspire against you. Since the dawn of air combat, men have strapped themselves to their air machines and taken on these deadly forces. You will quickly learn through playing Falcon that flying skill and aggressiveness count heavily in this contest but must be backed with knowledge and discipline. As in all contests that pit men against men, you must know the fundamentals of the game and be able to execute them. The Falcon computer simulation is a faithful re-creation of the air combat environment and, as such, requires the successful "pilot" to have training in the basics. Before we start our discussion of modern air warfare, let's look at where we've been.

Nothing and everything has changed in air combat since biplanes first appeared above the trenches of Europe and fought for control of the air. Nothing has changed in the character and traits of the men who fly and fight. The ground and the whiskey are both still hard, and the air is still mercilessly unforgiving of mistakes. Valor and clear thinking under pressure are still the stuff required when Falcon meets MiG, just as they were when Fokker fought Spad. Everything has changed, however, in the hardware of air combat. High technology has expanded weapon parameters and transformed aircraft performance to the point where air battles of today bear only a faint resemblance to those of the past.

DAWN PATROL

World War I started the era of air combat. Weapons and tactics that evolved in this war would affect aircraft design and air warfare throughout the rest of the century. The war started, as most wars do, with the warring nations fully prepared to fight the "last war." Most believed this would be a war of swift and decisive maneuver, led by the cavalry. The airplane, invented a mere decade prior to the outbreak of war, was not central to the strategy of either side. Things would soon change in the air and on the ground.

Enter the Machine Gun

On 5 October 1914 a French biplane called a Voisin patrolled above the battlefield performing routine reconnaissance. The Voisin's rear engine design gave the observer, Corporal Louis Quénault, a good view out the front of the aircraft and a clear field of fire for a newly installed Hotchkiss machine gun. On this day Corporal Quénault spotted the distinct silhouette and markings of a German Aviatik reconnaissance aircraft. The French Voisin, piloted by Joseph Frantz, closed to attack and at short range opened fire with the Hotchkiss gun. The Aviatik was caught completely by surprise, and spiraled into the ground mortally wounded. This first successful use of a machine gun on an airplane ushered in the era of air combat. Prior to this historic engagement, several unsuccessful attempts at shooting down aircraft had been made by the aircrews of both sides. Corporal Quénault's attack demonstrated that machine guns could be used in aerial combat to deny the enemy the use of the air. Figure 1-1 shows a two place pusher with a swivel-mounted gun similar to the one flown by Joseph Frantz and Louis Quénault.

By the end of 1914, aerial reconnaissance and artillery spotting had come to play an important role in the war effort. The swivel-mounted machine gun lead to an increase in air combat engagements as both sides fought to control the high ground above the trenches. It soon became clear that a better way had to be found to shoot at the enemy. Firing a movable machine gun from a moving aircraft at an uncooperative target proved to be a difficult task.

Fixed Machine Guns
Are Developed

Fixing the machine gun in place and pointing the entire aircraft was the first attempt to solve the problem. The French Nieuport 11 was one of the first aircraft to mount a fixed gun. Aircraft by this time were designed with front-mounted engines, and the Nieuport 11 solved the difficult problem

USAF Photographs from Office of TAC History Archives, HQ Tactical Air Command

Figure 1-1. Biplane pusher with swivel-mounted machine gun

of avoiding the propeller arc by placing the machine gun on the top of the upper wing. While this system was better, aiming this fixed gun was difficult due to the distance between the gun's perspective and the pilot's, and reloading was next to impossible.

The next big improvement came when a Frenchman named Roland Garros installed deflectors on the propellers of his plane and fired a machine gun with deadly accuracy through the propeller arc. Garros was downed by ground fire soon after he appeared on the battlefield with this new invention, and the Germans captured him and his aircraft. After examining the Garros airplane, Dutch aircraft designer Anthony Fokker worked with the Germans to perfect a synchronizer gear that allowed the machine gun to be fired through the propeller without the deflectors.

With the emergence of a lethal air-to-air weapon maneuverability became more important as fighter pilots strove to get into firing position

USAF Photographs from Office of TAC History Archives, HQ Tactical Air Command

Figure 1-2.   WWI fighter with fixed guns

on the enemy. Advances in aircraft and weapons continued throughout the rest of the war but the mold for fighter aircraft was cast. The successful practitioners of air warfare would possess maneuverable aircraft with fixed guns. This mold in many ways remains unchanged today. As you take to the air in the Falcon simulation, your aircraft is a true descendant of those first early fighters. Figure 1-2 shows a biplane fighter of this era.

The First Aerial Tactics

The role of aerial reconnaissance remained critical throughout the war, fueling the continued efforts on both sides to deny this strategy to the enemy. A pattern soon emerged where heavier and slower reconnaissance aircraft flew missions protected by smaller, more maneuverable fighter aircraft. Tactics to find and destroy the enemy were developed along with the basic principles and techniques of air combat.

These techniques where based on aircraft performance and air-to-air weapons just as they are today. The fixed, forward-firing machine gun had to be flown into lethal range, aimed, and fired. The gun attack, however, took time and some fine adjustments by the pilot. In order to have a reasonable chance for success it was best to get behind the opponent, in "the six o'clock" position, and shoot. This allowed more control, and you could stay in the envelope of the gun (the allowable firing parameter) for a longer period of time. Conversely, a head-on approach allowed you only a fleeting shot with no room for error, and presented the opponent with the same opportunity. As a result, offensive tactics centered on maneuvers that placed your aircraft in the six o'clock position of the enemy, and defensive tactics centered around keeping the enemy away from your six o'clock.

These fundamental fighter principles of offense and defense have changed little since World War I. Even in the current era of the all-aspect missile attack, you are still the most vulnerable to a close-in bandit at your six o'clock. From this position the enemy fighter can make multiple attacks and stay there to watch the results.

In any fighter aircraft there are large blind spots that restrict the vision of the pilot. Pilots soon learned that formations of mutually support-ing fighters could better their chances for survival by clearing these blind spots for each other. Fighters flying these first formations used hand signals to communicate.

The Fighter Pilot

Tactics were important, but tactics were just the means by which valiant men pursued this new form of warfare. At center stage was the fighter pilot. His fame was enhanced by the glamour and novelty of the flying machine, and further amplified because of the general public's disgust and horror of trench warfare. The press on both sides glorified the exploits of the aviators to direct public attention away from the war on the ground. The air war was portrayed as a chivalrous form of combat where the fighter pilots, like the knights of the round table, went forth at dawn to patrol the skies and joust the enemy one-on-one. This image would remain through-out the war and survive essentially intact through the wars that followed.

THE EXPANDING ENVELOPE

The bell for round one sounded, and the Great War in Europe ended. The potential of aerial warfare had been clearly demonstrated during World War I, even if that potential remained largely unfulfilled. In the next round of the war, air combat would have far-reaching effects on the outcome.

Blitzkrieg

Between the wars, continued advances in engines and aerodynamics led to new capabilities in combat aircraft. With these improvements aircraft could carry greater payloads and fly for longer distances. Tactics and doctrine soon developed to exploit these new capabilities and as World War II erupted, the airplane played a preeminent role.

In the conflict started with the debut of a new form of warfare called blitzkrieg. *Blitzkrieg* (also referred to as "lightning war") featured combined arms using mechanization, fire power, and mobility to defeat the enemy. These combined combat arms consisted of tanks, infantry, artillery, and, of course, airpower. The airplane, which had by now developed to embody both fire power and mobility, played the crucial role of attacking fixed enemy defenses and disrupting lines of communication and supply. The primary mission of the fighter aircraft was much the same as in the previous war: control the skies above the battlefield and provide cover for attacking aircraft and ground forces.

The Battle of Britain

Using the blitzkrieg, the German Army smashed through Poland and France and soon only the island nation of Great Britain stood in the way of complete victory. On 13 August 1940 the Germans unleashed *Adlertag* (Eagle Day), the air offensive against the British Isles. This offensive would clear the way for Operation Sea Lion, the invasion of England by the German Army. The Battle of Britain was fought in the ensuing months with the fate of the world in the balance.

The German Luftwaffe's goal was to destroy the British Royal Air Force (RAF) fighters in the air and on the ground. They started the operation by attacking RAF installations in the first months of the battle and then switched to bombing British cities. The Luftwaffe bombers carrying out these attacks where escorted by German fighters, and massive air battles developed as RAF fighters rose to oppose them. The Germans hoped to dominate the RAF in these big air battles and to create such heavy British losses that they could eventually control the skies. It was their own losses, however, that ended the battle. The RAF caused such high attrition on the attacking Germans that they had to stop fighting to prevent the destruction of the Luftwaffe.

The battle was a showcase for air power as the British Royal Air Force (RAF) blunted the German air offensive and thus the invasion. At the end of nearly a year of combat the RAF had lost 1,000 aircraft and the Luftwaffe close to 2,000. The British fighter pilot had emerged victoriously from the most important air battle in history.

Aircraft and Tactics

The aircraft used to fight the Battle of Britain and the rest of World War II were stamped from the same mold as the biplane fighters of the previous war. Improved forward-firing machine guns and cannons gave these aircraft a more deadly armament package but the basic approach to air combat remained the same. The name of the game was still to maneuver your aircraft to the six o'clock position of your opponent and open fire with your guns. The effective range of these new guns had doubled since the previous air war but the need to keep control of your opponent and remain in firing range had not changed.

Improved aircraft maneuverability increased the aerodynamic envelope or boundaries of aerial combat. More powerful aircraft could generate higher G turns and fly faster and higher than the fighters of the previous war. When an aircraft changes direction, acceleration is produced. This acceleration is known to fighter pilots as Gs (pronounced gees). When you're sitting at your computer playing Falcon, you are pulling 1G. When an aircraft such as an F-16 enters a combat turn, it can pull up to 9Gs. This means your body is slammed by nine times the force of gravity. Imagine trying to lift your arms or turn your head under these loads. World War II saw the advent of fighters that could perform 5G turns and although this is only about half of what a modern fighter can do, it was still a big change over the fighters of World War I. Fighter pilots were subjected to increased levels of violent motion, flying combat maneuvers in these more powerful aircraft. In addition to increased G force, combat speeds more than doubled between the wars, which reduced the reaction time of the fighter pilot by one half. Life and death decisions were time-compressed as fighters closed at up to ten miles a minute.

Mutual Support

A less dramatic, but equally important change in fighter aircraft was the introduction of the radio. The addition of the radio had a profound impact on fighter tactics during this period. The radio allowed interaircraft communication which meant the concept of mutual supporting aircraft could now be refined. The use of the radio gave birth to specific formations with firmly established positions and responsibilities. While many different formations evolved, they where all based on providing supporting fire power and more complete visibility for sighting enemy aircraft. The concept of one offensive fighter and a supporting wingman with defensive responsibilities was introduced in World War I, perfected in World War II, and is still used today. Figure 1-3 shows P-51 Mustangs flying in mutual support formation.

Fighting Spirit

On a fall day in 1943, Francis "Gabby" Gabreski was leading a section of P-47 fighters of the famous 56th Fighter Group. Their mission was to provide escort for B-17 bombers. After entering enemy territory, Gabreski sighted a formation of heavily armed, twin engine Me-110 German fighters maneuvering to attack the B-17s. Flying cover for the Me-110 were the more maneuverable Me-109s and Focke-Wulf-190 fighters. Without hesitation Gabreski dove into the Me-110s, breaking up their attack and disrupting the formation. He quickly closed to inside 300 feet of one of the

USAF Photographs from Office of TAC History Archives, HQ Tactical Air Command

Figure 1-3. WWII P-51s flying mutual support

cumbersome Me-110s and tore it to pieces with the P-47's eight .50 caliber machine guns. Unfortunately the enemy plane exploded at close range and Gabreski's P-47 got hit by the debris. Pulling away from the fireball in his damaged aircraft, he noticed another Me-110 making a firing pass on the B-17s. Again he closed with the enemy and shot down the would-be attacker. The other members of his section provided support during this engagement by holding off the escorting German fighters while Gabreski made his second attack with a damaged airplane in an area filled with enemy fighters. Figure 1-4 shows a P-47 similar to the plane flown by "Gabby."

The fighting spirit of the World War II fighter pilot was exemplified by men like Gabreski. As in past battles, it was men like him who provided

USAF Photographs from Office of TAC History Archives, HQ Tactical Air Command

Figure 1-4.   P-47

the winning margin. (As a footnote, the 56th Fighter Group is now the 56th
Tactical Training Wing flying the F-16 Falcon.)

The First Jet Fighter

In the summer of 1944, a British pilot flying a reconnaissance mission in
his twin engine Mosquito bomber came under attack by a strange new
German aircraft. This aircraft had no propeller and flew at an incredible
speed. The British pilot dove into nearby cloud cover to avoid being shot
down and returned to base to report the encounter. This was the first
recorded jet aerial combat, and the jet aircraft in this engagement turned

out to be the 580-mph German Me-262. This speed was remarkable considering one of the fastest fighters of the war, the American P-51 Mustang, could fly at only 450 mph. During the war the Germans, British, and Americans had all been designing jet-powered aircraft but the German Me-262 was the first successful operational jet fighter.

Fortunately for the allies, the Me-262 was plagued by development problems that limited its effectiveness. Hitler insisted that the aircraft be used as a bomber and this delayed development and restricted the number used as fighters. The primary performance advantages it possessed over other aircraft did not have a significant impact in the bomber role. This advantage could have made a difference in the aircraft-versus-aircraft combat arena if large numbers of Me-262s had arrived earlier in the war and been used as fighters. The daylight bombing of German cities may have been stopped by the Me-262 but too few of the fighter versions arrived too late in the war to make a difference in the outcome. Nevertheless, this first jet fighter signaled the coming of a new age in air combat.

World War II ended with Hiroshima, and the contribution of the fighter pilot to the war effort became the stuff of legends. Prime Minister Winston Churchill in a speech to the British people paid tribute to the RAF pilots of the Battle of Britain by saying, "Never in the field of human conflict was so much owed by so many to so few." The fighter pilot and his aircraft had for the first time played a central role in the outcome of a major war.

JET COMBAT OVER MANCHURIA

Five years after the end of the Second World War a new page in the history of air combat was written. On 25 June 1950 the North Korean Army struck south across the 38th Parallel, the border between North and South Korea, and within days the first operational U.S. jet fighters saw action. The early engagements of the war pitted these U.S. jets against Soviet-built, piston-powered aircraft until November 8, 1950. On that day, an F80, piloted by Lt. Russell J. Brown, shot down a MiG-15 fighter, and the era of jet-versus-jet combat began.

In the five years between the wars, the Soviet Union and the United States along with Great Britain, France, and Sweden all raced to exploit captured German jet fighter technology. Although most of these countries possessed their own jet aircraft development programs, they did not have the German operational experience and technological base. The Korean War started with the U.S. and the Soviet Union firmly out in front in fighter design. The U.S. F-86 Sabre and the Soviet MiG-15 were the best fighters of this period and featured jet engines coupled with another German innovation, the swept-back wing. This design opened up new speed and altitude regimes in air combat. The F-86 is shown in Figure 1-5.

USAF Photographs from Office of TAC History Archives, HQ Tactical Air Command

Figure 1-5.   F-86s

USAF Photographs from Office of TAC History Archives, HQ Tactical Air Command

Figure 1-6. MiG-15

Air Superiority

The air war in Korea started with U.S. ground attack fighters and heavy bombers flying missions in support of the ground war. The communist forces soon introduced Soviet-built jet fighters in an attempt to disrupt this effort, setting the stage for a classic air showdown between the F-86 and the MiG-15 for control of the skies over Korea. In the first few engagements, the U.S. pilots learned that the MiG-15 was in many ways superior to the Sabre. Its jet engine could take it to higher altitudes giving it an advantage at the start of the fight. Figure 1-6 is a Soviet-built MiG-15.

This performance advantage, however, was not enough to offset the superior training and experience of the U.S. Air Force fighter pilots, many of whom had fought in World War II. Even though the MiG-15 was in many ways a better airplane than the F-86, the air war quickly turned into a one-sided contest with the F-86 gaining air superiority over the entire region. This *top cover* over the battlefield allowed U.S. bombers a free hand at striking the enemy. In one month the U.S. Air Force shot down 77 MiG-15s without the loss of a single F-86. The final numbers were approximately 815 MiG-15s destroyed in air combat to a loss of 78 F-86s, a staggering 10 to 1 kill ratio.

Lessons Learned

Jet combat in Korea was in some ways similar to the air war of World War II. The gun was the sole air-to-air weapon and it still dictated tactics and maneuvers. The .50 caliber machine gun that was so effective in World War II, however, proved to be inadequate in jet combat. Jet aircraft had harder metal structures making them difficult to kill with the .50 caliber gun. American pilots soon noticed that they were hitting MiGs but not destroying them. In addition, aerial gunnery had become more difficult due to the increase in aircraft speeds and turn rates. The fighter pilot needed a higher caliber gun with a better system of aiming. Cannons were first introduced on fighters in World War II but it was not until Korea that they became a necessity.

Cannons are higher caliber guns with a heavier projectile. The use of a cannon usually meant a slower rate of fire. Before the first jet-versus-jet combat it was thought that smaller caliber guns with high fire rates were more lethal in air-to-air combat. During this war it was learned that a jet needed a gun with a high fire rate and a larger projectile. The F-86 fought with the .50 caliber machine gun for most of the war, and over 1,000 enemy aircraft escaped after being hit by .50 caliber rounds. The U.S. Air Force might have doubled the number of MiG kills if the F-86 had been equipped with a cannon with a high rate of fire.

Aiming the gun was another story. Jet combat highlighted the need for a system to help the pilot hit a high-speed target. Fighter pilots in the Korean War found it difficult to estimate the required lead angle on the target without an accurate range input to the gun sight. Their gun sights were similar to the ones used in the previous war, which gave the pilot a solution based on a fixed-range assumption. Greater turn rates and the increased pace of jet combat made these gun sights obsolete. Aircraft radars were being introduced during this period, and designers started to incorporate the use of ranging radars into fighter gun sights to solve the aiming problem. Unguided rockets were also being developed in an effort to improve air-to-air weapon lethality. While none of these efforts made a significant contribution to the air war in Korea, they did begin a new trend in fighter design.

The Korean War introduced the first jet-versus-jet combat but it had more in common with the air wars of the past than it had with the next era in air combat. Most tactics developed in the first two wars were used successfully in the Korean War. The fighter pilot had to find the enemy visually, close to the six o'clock position, and shoot him down. Speeds had created a more demanding environment but this basic air combat goal remained the same. Korea also reinforced the universal truth that the man in the cockpit dictates the outcome of air warfare; differences in fighter pilots count far more than differences in airplanes.

A NEW DIRECTION

A multitude of fighter designs took to the air in the years after the Korean War. This was a time when aircraft technology was achieving new breakthroughs, and speed and altitude barriers were falling almost weekly. Missile technology had finally produced new types of air-to-air weapons and some "experts" wrongly predicted the marriage of missiles and supersonic jets would result in the end of the "dog fight" or maneuvering air-to-air engagement. If air-to-air fighting was necessary, they theorized, missiles would be used to destroy enemy aircraft without the need to maneuver at close range. Some tacticians further concluded that all air-to-air combat would be just a sideshow to the real battle that would take place in the next war; toe-to-toe nuclear combat.

This next war would be fought with nuclear missiles and bombs, said theorists, and the fighters' primary purpose would be to conduct short-range nuclear attack missions or to shoot down nuclear bombers attacking the United States. The fighter force structure that appeared in the decade following the Korean War was built around these two ideas. Speed was considered important in fighter design but maneuverability suffered as fighters grew bigger and heavier in order to carry nuclear bombs or an intercept radar. The F-105 fighter was designed for high-speed, low-altitude nuclear attack. This aircraft is an example of a heavy aircraft with a clean aerodynamic design. This design produced speed and payload capability at the expense of maneuverability. The theories that formed the basis for our post-Korean fighter force would not withstand the test of combat.

The Red River Rats

The Vietnam War quickly showed that our predictions of future air combat were mistaken. Vietnam was a limited war like the war in Korea but the similarities ended there. The Vietnam War pushed the United States and the world into a new age of air combat and clearly demonstrated the strength of air power in the modern age.

The air war in Vietnam was divided into two parts: the war in the South and the war in the North across the Red River. The war in North Vietnam pitted airplanes for the first time against an integrated air defense system consisting of fighters, *Surface to Air Missiles* (SAMs) and *Anti-Aircraft Artillery* (AAA). The American fighter pilots who flew missions into the North called themselves the Red River Rats, and they fought a new kind of aerial warfare.

The objective of the air war over the North was to disrupt the war-making effort of the North Vietnamese and curtail their ability to supply communist forces in the South. Shortly after the U.S. started bombing military targets in North Vietnam, Soviet-supplied MiGs, SAMs, and AAA appeared and a new phase in air warfare began. The F-105 carried most of the bombing load early in the war and it was soon apparent that its lack of maneuverability made it vulnerable to MiGs. The Soviets had followed an evolutionary path to fighter development, and during the Vietnam War introduced the MiG-17,19, and 21. These fighters lacked the sophisticated avionics and range of American fighters but were highly maneuverable and formidable adversaries in the air defense role. The U.S. Air Force did not have an air fighter to protect the F-105s and soon turned to the recently developed Navy F-4 Phantom. The Air Force had been looking for a flexible multirole fighter before the war in Vietnam began and found that the F-4 Phantom, shown in Figure 1-7, was the best choice to fill this role.

USAF Photographs from Office of TAC History Archives, HQ Tactical Air Command

Figure 1-7.   F-4

The Navy had developed the F-4 for the primary mission of fleet air defense and it was not a true air superiority fighter. It did, however, have excellent avionics and armament that included advanced radar and the new Sparrow and Sidewinder air-to-air missiles. In addition the F-4 could carry a big bomb load and had the best *thrust to weight ratio* of any fighter of the period. The first versions of the F-4 were not equipped with a gun because it was assumed the gun would not be used in the new age of air-to-air missile combat.

There is no question that the U.S. won the air war in Vietnam. American forces quickly developed countermeasures and tactics to deal with the SAMs, AAA, and MiGs, and only political decisions limited the effectiveness of the air campaign. Before the end of the war the Red River Rats disabled the North Vietnamese. Even so, U.S. forces did not dominate the war in air-to-air combat as they had in the Korean war. Table 1-1 shows

Table 1-1.   Vietnam Air Combat Results (1965-1975)

	MiG-17	MiG-19	MiG-21	TOTALS
COMBINED US FORCES USAF/USN/USMC				
SHOT DOWN	96	10	87	193
SHOT DOWN BY	28	6	47	87
KILL RATIO 2.4 : 1				

the final air combat results of American fighters against their MiG counterparts.

Lessons Relearned

The final 2.4 to 1 kill ratio was a testimony to our lack of emphasis and poor training in air-to-air combat. The F-4 Phantom was not a lightweight air superiority fighter like the F-86 of the Korean War but it was more than a match for the MiG-21 when flown correctly. The air war in Vietnam showed that the missile was an effective air-to-air weapon but it did not change the need for fighter pilots to know basic air combat fundamentals. In fact, the increased thrust to weight ratio of the F-4 and its new types of air-to-air armament increased the amount of training required.

The F-4 could maneuver in the vertical (go straight up) better than any aircraft of the war. Maneuvering in the vertical gave the F-4 an advantage over the MiGs but it took training and practice to master this type of fight. The MiGs could out turn the Phantom and had better slow-speed handling qualities so the F-4 pilot had to know how to exploit these advantages. Training was equally important in air-to-air weaponry because the Sparrow and Sidewinder missiles were complicated and required in-depth knowledge to employ correctly. The gun was also rediscovered as an air-to-air weapon and accounted for about 30 percent of the MiG kills of the war. We will discuss Falcon air-to-air weapons in detail later in this book. The weapons used by the Falcon are direct descendants of the Vietnam era missiles and guns.

The primary lesson learned in the air war in Vietnam was that as aircraft complexity increased, so did training requirements. Fighter pilots in this new era of air combat would require intense realistic training to master the specialized aircraft and the demanding environment. The missile age had not changed the fundamental rules of air combat; it had just added new rules to the list.

THE F-16 FIGHTING FALCON

2

"Rove your allotted area, find the enemy and
shoot him down...anything else is rubbish."

—Baron Von Richthofen

"Viper 21 snap 350 degrees, bandits at 25 miles committing south."
    "Roger Red Top, Viper is coming to a heading of 350."
    "Red Top, Viper 21 has two contacts on the nose, 22 miles, angels 20."
    "Those contacts are your targets Viper."

The fight was on. The mission, a two-versus-two training sortie against the F-5 Aggressors, was now down to a one-versus-two due to a ground abort by my wingman. The F-5s were simulating North Korean MiG-21s flying an attack mission while I was flying point defense. *Point defense* requires a fighter to protect a specific point such as an airfield. Since you are tied to that point, you do not have the flexibility to engage targets of choice, and you must abide by strict engagement criteria so you don't get stripped away from the assets you are defending. The "MiGs" were trying to get past my Combat Air Patrol (CAP) to attack my "airfield." For this mission the Ground Control Intercept (GCI) facility, with the call sign of Red Top, had the job of calling bandits that got within 25 NM (nautical miles) of the CAP position. Ground radar cannot provide detailed target information but can cover a much wider range than a fighter's radar; ground radar can search 360 degrees and give the fighter pilot a bearing and range to the target. Most fighter radar, such as the APG-66 in the F-16, can only search 120 degrees in azimuth. Once they find a target, they can provide the pilot with more detailed information such as target heading, aspect, airspeed, and altitude. GCI is important in a point-defense role because the people in GCI watch all of the avenues of attack and point you in the right direction once a target meets the commit criteria. In this mission we were using a simple range commit of 25 NM.

When Red Top gave me a bearing and range to the targets I took control of the intercept, powered up to 500 knots, and turned towards the sun to get the offset from the bandits. By taking displacement "up sun" (into the sun), you force the bad guys to look into the sun to find you. At 10 NM I switched the radar from search to single-target track and locked on to the trailing bandit in the formation. At the same time I turned to place the bandits on the nose (to face them head-on). This made my airplane very difficult to see because a fighter aircraft has the smallest visual cross section when it is pointing directly at you. As the targets came to the nose, the Target Designator (TD) box in the Heads Up Display (HUD) came into view. Within seconds I got a tally-ho (visual sighting) on one of the F-5s. As the range closed I spotted the other F-5; it was obvious they did not see me as I started a conversion to their six o'clock. My presence was a complete surprise as I closed the range and called a "Lima" shot (Aim-9L Sidewinder) on the trailing F-5. Five seconds later I called, "Lima kill on the trailing F-5, heading 140 degrees at angels 20." Standard Rules of Engagement (ROE) call for missile shots to be spaced five seconds apart to approximate a missile's flight time. If you were firing a real missile you would shoot and watch to see if it hit the target, and then fire again if it missed. In this fight any two missile shots, five seconds apart, resulted in a kill. As I was calling the kill shot, both F-5s started a 7G break turn into me. The trailing F-5 must have heard my kill shot relayed by his GCI because he fell out of formation and did an aileron roll to signal he was dead. The lead F-5 kept turning hard into me and was soon too close for a missile shot. I pulled the nose to lead pursuit and cut across the circle for a gun shot. At about 2,500 feet the F-5 pilot maneuvered wildly to avoid becoming the star of my gun camera film. Fighter pilots call this maneuver the "funky chicken" or the "guns jink." In air combat you occasionally need to perform one of the many unpleasant gun attack defenses known collectively by this term. Gun defense requires swift aircraft movement to change your plane of motion. The specifics of this defense will be covered later in the book but these maneuvers are normally very sudden and violent. Of course the alternative to a guns jink is to get torn apart by a Soviet 23-mm cannon, which is even more violent. Even though this particular Aggressor pilot was suffering terribly during his wild maneuvering, it wasn't enough to save him. I called, "guns kill on the F-5 at 13,000 feet" and shortly after he aileron rolled. The fight was over.

As an aside, any time you call a kill on another fighter pilot you must have it documented by gun camera film. Even though fighter pilots are of the highest integrity, they have been known to exaggerate when it comes to air-to-air gunnery. If you cannot back up a kill shot with film, or if you fire out of parameters, you owe five dollars to the guy you mistakenly removed from the fight.

It was my first fight against the F-5 Aggressors in the F-16. My squadron had converted from F-4s only two months before and I was still getting used to the airplane. This fight lasted about four minutes total, and I had "killed" both F-5s. The next two engagements ended the same way, a feat unheard of in the tired, old F-4 Phantom. I had fought one of those same Aggressor pilots about nine months earlier, and had spent most of my time looking over my shoulder at the business end of the F-5. I was shocked at how lame the performance of the dreaded Aggressors seemed when flown against the F-16. These same guys had terrorized my F-4 squadron the previous year, and now they looked like the rookies' auxiliary flying club.

The Aggressors squadrons were formed after the Vietnam War as a direct result of the mediocre U.S. kill ratio. These squadrons exist to train the operational fighter squadrons in air-to-air combat. They are manned by highly experienced pilots who study enemy tactics. When we fought the Aggressors in our F-4s we won some and we lost some, with the Aggressors losing a few less. After several months in the F-16 it became clear that the tables had turned, and we rarely lost to an F-5. Losses did happen occasionally (even a blind squirrel sometimes finds a nut), but as a rule we

USAF Photographs from Office of TAC History Archives, HQ Tactical Air Command

Figure 2-1.   F-16 climbing straight up

dominated the air-to-air engagements with the Aggressors. Figure 2-1 shows an F-16 climbing straight up. Figure 2-2 is of F-5 Aggressor aircraft.

USAF Photographs from Office of TAC History Archives, HQ Tactical Air Command

Figure 2-2. F-5 Aggressors

THE FALCON IS BORN

The conversion of U.S. Air Force fighter squadrons from the F-4 to the F-16 highlighted a dramatic new direction in fighter philosophy that was born out of the Vietnam experience. The F-16 development program came about primarily through the fortuitous combination of several forces.

MiG Scare

In July of 1967 at the Domodedovo airfield near Moscow, several new Soviet fighters were displayed for the first time to the Western press. The two aircraft that made the biggest impact and caused the greatest concern were the MiG-23 Flogger and the MiG-25 Foxbat.

The MiG-23 had variable sweep wings and a sleek aerodynamic design. It was the follow-up to the formidable MiG-21 Fishbed that the North Vietnamese were using so effectively against the F-4. The F-4 had a range and armament advantage over the Fishbed but the F-4's new air-to-air missiles had not obviated the need for maneuverability. In this area the MiG-21 had a clear advantage. The MiG-23 and 25 took the advantage farther with better range, and armament that included air-to-air missiles of the same type carried by the F-4. In addition to these improvements, the MiG-23 was even faster than the MiG-21. Figure 2-3 shows the MiG-23.

Figure 2-4 shows the MiG-25 Foxbat. The appearance of the MiG-25 at Domodedovo did for U.S. fighter development what the appearance of Sputnik did for the U.S. space program. The Foxbat was a large twin engine fighter with unprecedented performance; the West had no fighter aircraft that could fly as fast or as high. In addition, the Foxbat was equipped with new high-powered radar and long-range air-to-air missiles. The introduction of this jet by the Soviets sent tremors through the American fighter community. Almost a decade after the Foxbat was first displayed to the West, a Russian pilot defected with a Foxbat and landed in Japan. Careful analysis of the aircraft by the U.S. intelligence community proved some of our fears to be unfounded. It did not have the ability to fly at high speeds at medium or low altitudes as we had first postulated, and it was not a very maneuverable jet. The conclusion of the Foxbat analysis, however, was that it was a remarkable fighter in the very high-altitude, high-speed regimes in which it was designed to operate.

In the early 1960s the U.S. Air Force had begun to investigate design options for a true air superiority fighter along the lines of the P-51 Mustang and F-86 Sabre. The project was designated Fighter Experimental (or FX), and was moving at a snail's pace until the Soviets unveiled their new fighters at Domodedovo. The Foxbat was especially troublesome because

USAF Photographs from Office of TAC History Archives, HQ Tactical Air Command

Figure 2-3.   MiG-23 Flogger

USAF Photographs from Office of TAC History Archives, HQ Tactical Air Command

Figure 2-4.   MiG-25 Foxbat

its estimated altitude and speed performance made it invulnerable to the mainstay of the Air Force, the F-4 Phantom. The FX project was injected with new energy after the Foxbat was unveiled, and parameters for the new fighter were developed to make the FX superior to the perceived Foxbat threat.

The Lightweight Fighter

During the early stages of the FX project in the mid 1960s another concept emerged called the *Advanced Day Fighter* (ADF). This concept called for a smaller aircraft that could outperform the MiG-21, and yet be cheaper and simpler than the FX. The appearance of the Foxbat put the ADF concept on hold and a new FX called the F-15 went forward as the highest priority Air Force fighter project. As the F-15 project got under way, the Air Force realized that its high cost and complexity would limit the number of F-15s produced. The cost for the F-15 and the new Navy fighter, the F-14, were five times higher than the previous generation of fighters: 2 million for the F-4 versus 10 million for either the F-14 or F-15. A new approach to competitive prototyping was introduced by Deputy Secretary of Defense David A. Packard to reverse the trend of large, high-cost fighters. The ADF, now called the Lightweight Fighter (LWF) project, was the front-running candidate for this new approach to aircraft development. This procurement strategy called for creating several fighter aircraft designs to meet broad objectives rather than a single design to meet exact specifications.

The cost of the F-15 had soared in response to the need for a long-range air-to-air radar and high Mach capability to fight against the Foxbat. The LWF would be free of having to meet specific military operational needs such as these, and would be allowed to pursue advanced technological options in fighter design. The different fighter designs would then be flown in competition to determine which, if any, should be bought. General Dynamics and Northrop won the initial contracts to build prototypes, and the YF-16 and YF-17 were developed. (The *Y* in the prefix of the designation was used instead of the classic *X* to denote that the aircraft was not purely an experimental design but a combination of new and off-the-shelf technology.) The *Y* was dropped after the YF-16 won the fly-off competition and entered production.

USAF Photographs from Office of TAC History Archives, HQ Tactical Air Command

Figure 2-5. YF-16 chased by F-4

Both teams produced unique designs to accomplish the same goal of producing a small, maneuverable fighter aircraft. The General Dynamics YF-16, shown being chased by the less maneuverable Phantom F-4 in Figure 2-5, had a single engine, complete fly-by-wire flight controls, a side-stick controller, and a 30 degree reclined seat. In addition, it was the first fighter to feature relaxed static stability, which allowed the horizontal tail to produce an upward lift vector to aid in turning the aircraft. (A conventional aircraft such as the F-15 and the YF-17 possessed static stability, which required the tail to produce a downward lift vector. This hindered turning ability.) The Northrop YF-17 was a twin engine aircraft with partial fly-by-wire flight controls, a conventional center-control stick, and distinctive twin vertical tails.

The differences between the two aircraft were primarily of form rather than function. Both were highly maneuverable aircraft with similar range and payload capabilities. The competition was close but the General Dynamics YF-16 pulled ahead in cost, range, acceleration, and turning ability near the supersonic speed range. During flight testing of the prototypes, the Air Force announced that the winning aircraft would go into full-scale production to become the low-end fighter in the new high/low air combat concept.

The High/Low Mix

The high/low mix concept was developed by the Air Force in response to the growing trend to produce large, complicated, and costly fighters, such as the F-15, that could only be produced in small quantities. The high/low mix was a brave attempt by the Air Force to stand up and face the reality of air combat. This reality, known intuitively by fighter pilots, is that numbers count more than aircraft capability—that is, you can beat superior odds with superior aircraft and training only to a certain point. After that point the side with the largest number of fighters will win. The trend toward a small number of very capable aircraft might be yet another concept that would not survive the test of combat.

The post-Vietnam leadership in the Air Force considered quantity, cost, and aircraft capabilities and concluded that because the F-16 costs less, enough of them could be produced to make the high/low mix strategy work. The F-16 was a very capable fighter but it was not equipped with long-range radar or a radar-guided air-to-air missile. The F-15/F-16 mix would allow sufficient numbers and complementary capabilities. Both aircraft were maneuverable, but the F-16 was slightly more so. Both aircraft had good weapon systems, but the F-15's had the advantage. The F-14 is in the same size and performance class as the F-15.

A final word about the high/low mix philosophy and the F-16: The concept proved to be successful, but in a different way from what was originally envisioned. Over the last decade the F-16 evolved from a pure low-cost, lightweight fighter to a multipurpose aircraft similar in many ways to the F-4. This evolution was brought about by two major factors. The first was the aircraft's great flexibility to adapt to a wide range of fighter missions. The second was the relative low cost of the F-16, which allowed it to be bought in sufficient numbers to have an impact. The high/low mix strategy now involves having a small number of expensive aircraft for specialized missions—such as the F-15E for all-weather day/night attack—and a large number of lower- cost multimission aircraft.

The Winner

In January of 1975, Secretary of the Air Force John McLucas announced that the YF-16 had won the competition. An order for the first 15 aircraft soon followed. The first operational F-16s were sent to the 388th Tactical Fighter Wing at Hill AFB in Utah in January of 1979. By the end of 1980 the 388th had been equipped with over 100 F-16s. This Wing had four squadrons, two of which were assigned training duties while the other two became combat ready. The 56th Tactical Training Wing at MacDill AFB in Florida received the F-16 shortly thereafter, and became the primary training Wing with four training squadrons. The Air Force then began the task of replacing overseas F-4 units with the F-16. The first overseas Wing to get the F-16 was the Eighth Tactical Fighter Wing (the Wolf Pack) stationed in Kunsan Air Base in the Republic of Korea. I was assigned to this Wing and flying the F-4D until the Wing converted to the F-16.

Falcons in Combat

The F-16 proved to be a powerful aircraft with capabilities that dwarfed its predecessor, the F-4. This superiority, however, was not apparent at first glance, and several Air Force Wing Commanders in Europe expressed reluctance to convert from the F-4 to the F-16. They concluded that the aircraft's small size meant limited range and payload when in fact the F-16 could fly farther than the F-4 with as many bombs, and deliver them with three times the accuracy. They were also concerned that the F-16 did not possess a radar-guided missile. While this was a valid concern, the Sparrow radar guided-missile carried by the F-4 was largely ineffective when fighting at low altitudes. While the F-4's radar and the Sparrow missile had severe constraints in the low-altitude clutter environment, the pulse-Doppler radar in the F-16 could find targets at low altitude and the new all-aspect Sidewinder missile could engage and kill them. In addition, the small size and unmatched maneuverability of the Falcon made it the best air-to-air fighter in the world.

All of these capabilities where quickly discerned by American and NATO operational fighter squadrons as they gained experience in the aircraft. On 7 June 1981 any further doubts about the F-16 were laid to rest when the Israelis bombed the Iraqi nuclear reactor at Osirak. Six F-15s escorted eight bomb-carrying F-16s that attacked and destroyed the target in a daring daylight raid, effectively demonstrating the air-to-ground prowess of the Falcon. A year later these same Israeli F-16s were used in Lebanon's Bekaa valley to win air superiority. In this conflict the F-16 and F-15 combined to produce a lopsided Israeli victory over the Syrian MiG-21s and MiG-23s. The final box score for this conflict gave the F-16 a slight numerical edge, 44 kills to the F-15's 40 kills, with neither aircraft suffering any losses. The value of the lightweight fighter concept, as embodied by the F-16, was clear to the world.

THE F-16 FIGHTING FALCON

Before we examine the Falcon's design, let's clear up some of the confusion associated with the F-16's name. When the F-16 arrived at Hill AFB it was still unnamed. I arrived at Hill in late summer of 1981, when the airplane was being called "Viper" by the fighter pilots who flew it. The name caught on. Several months later when I had returned to Korea, the Air Force officially named the jet the "Fighting Falcon"—a name generally disliked by most of the fighter jocks flying the airplane. The name "Falcon" was OK, but the word "fighting" seemed out of place and redundant as the name of a fighter aircraft. As it turned out, the French had already used the Falcon name on a commercial transport jet; the Air Force added the "Fighting" part to the name to distinguish it from the French aircraft. The Air Force evidently wanted to stick with names of birds for fighters so the "Viper" name faded with the years, and only a few of us still use it. Nobody but paper-pushing pentagon staff officers ever uses the first word in the official name for the F-16. The jets are called the "sixteen" or the "Falcon" by the guys that drive them.

USAF Photographs from Office of TAC History Archives, HQ Tactical Air Command

Figure 2-6.   F-16 strakes

The Airframe

The most striking feature of the F-16 is its blended body fuselage. This concept, called *wing body blending,* requires the wing to gradually get thicker until it "blends" with the fuselage of the aircraft. The fuselage is shaped to look and perform like a wing, which enables the aircraft to have smaller wings, saving weight and cost. Figure 2-6 shows the blended body of the F-16, and another feature of the F-16 airframe—the strakes. *Strakes* are thin wing-like extensions that stretch from the wings to the cockpit area on both sides of the F-16. The strakes produce *vortices* (high energy air flow) that give the jet stability at a high angle of attack. The F-16 gets a large measure of its performance from these strakes and from the leading edge flaps. The *leading edge flaps* are high-lift devices on the front (or leading edge) of the wing. These flaps are programmed by the flight control computer to extend at certain angles of attack, which improves the turning ability of the F-16.

The Engine

The power of the F-16 is directly related to the power of the Pratt & Whitney F100 engine. The engine is an axial-flow turbo fan engine that produces approximately 25,000 pounds of thrust in afterburner and 15,000 pounds in military power (the highest non-afterburning thrust setting). The F100 achieves this remarkable performance partly through breakthroughs in metallurgy that allow extreme temperatures in the engine's core, and a corresponding higher thrust. The temperature in the core of the F100 is hotter by over 700 degrees Fahrenheit than the J79 engine that powered the F-4.

Another important feature of this engine is the turbo fan design. In a turbo fan engine the fan section is comprised of a series of large blades in the very front of the engine. These blades are powered by combustion in the core or hot section of the engine. As the fan turns, it pushes air into the engine. Most of this air goes into the main engine section to be compressed, mixed with fuel, and ignited—causing a violent expansion and thrust that powers the aircraft (and also turns the fan). The remaining air is propelled by the fan to go around (or bypass) the core of the engine and when expelled, creates additional thrust. This bypass air makes the engine very fuel efficient. Because of the turbo fan F100 engine, the F-16 has excellent range despite its small size.

The F100 engine gives an F-16 that is configured for air-to-air combat a thrust to weight ratio of one to one, resulting in a high sustained turn rate and excellent acceleration. In addition, you do not need the afterburner to take off in the F-16, as you do in the F-4.

The Eye of the Falcon

A wise, gnarled old F-4 backseater of mine once said, "Pete, nothing good will ever happen to you in air combat without detection." F-4 backseaters, or "pitters" as they're called, are known for their nerves of steel and sage advice. The job of a pitter in an F-4 is to operate the radar and other weapon systems and to keep "the stick actuator" (the pilot) out of trouble. Detection of the enemy *is* critical in both air-to-air and air-to-ground missions. The F-16 is equipped with the Westinghouse APG-66 pulse-Doppler radar.

Pulse-Doppler radar has the primary job of helping you find enemy fighters before they find you. It can do this at all altitudes, and its pulse-Doppler design allows you to detect low-flying targets in ground clutter. Before the advent of pulse-Doppler radar, the low-altitude regime was a safe place for enemy fighters to hide. Aircraft such as the F-4 were susceptible to ambush even with powerful radar systems because older radar could not detect bandits flying close to the ground. In the F-4, we flew low-level ground attack training missions and rarely picked up attacking bandits on radar. (Most were smart enough to attack from low altitudes.) We would normally spot attackers for the first time at our six o'clock position closing for a shot. After converting to the F-16, we flew nearly the same ground-attack profiles but instead of being ambushed by the bad guys we would ambush them. The APG-66 radar allowed us to "see" the bandits on radar long before they could find our F-16s visually. This gave us the offensive even though we were flying ground-attack missions. In this era of the deadly all-aspect air-to-air missile, you are either on the offensive or you're just a target waiting to be blown out of your cockpit. The APG-66 allows you keep all of your body parts in their correct position. The Falcon simulation replicates this deadly environment and to be successful at the fame, it is imperative that you learn how to use the radar.

The secondary purpose of the radar is to assist the pilot in bombing and navigating. The APG-66 has several air-to-ground modes that allow the pilot to drop accurate bombs. In these modes the radar provides ranging information to the target, and feeds this data to the Fire Control and Navigation Panel (FCNP). The FCNP then computes a bomb solution and presents the information to the pilot in the Heads Up Display (HUD). The accuracy of this system was demonstrated during the Israeli raid on the nuclear reactor at Osirak. The Falcons dropped 2000lb dumb (unguided) bombs using on-board avionics, and destroyed the reactor dome without causing collateral damage. When word of the attack was reported in the press it was assumed that the bombs used were laser guided due to the surgical precision of the strike. It took several months before the press would believe that an aircraft could drop dumb bombs with that kind of

USAF Photographs from Office of TAC History Archives, HQ Tactical Air Command

Figure 2-7. F-16 carrying Mk-84s and Sidewinders

accuracy. Figure 2-7 shows an F-16 carrying Mk-84 2000lb bombs and Sidewinder air-to- air missiles.

Electronic Combat

Electronic combat is the use of the electromagnetic spectrum to wage war. Electronic combat for the purposes of our discussion will refer only to the use of Threat Warning Systems (TWS) to detect radar emissions, and passive and active jamming of radar and Infrared (IR) threat systems.

The F-16 has a TWS called the ALR-69, which detects radar emissions and displays them to the pilot. Once the pilot realizes that he is under attack, the F-16 has a chaff and flare dispensing system called the ALE-40 that can be used to decoy radar and IR guided missiles. *Chaff* consists of metallic strips that reflect radar energy and present false targets to enemy radars. *Flares* imitate the red-hot engine exhaust of the F-16 and decoy IR guided missiles. The ALR-69 and the ALE-40 are referred to as passive systems since they do not actively transmit energy from the aircraft to the threat system. In addition to these passive systems, the Falcon can carry several types of Electronic Counter Measures (ECM) pods that actively transmit energy to jam enemy radars.

The great military tactician Sun Tzu Wu wrote, "All warfare is based on deception." The Falcon is well-equipped to fight Electronic Combat, which is nothing more than the ancient concept of deception applied to the modern battlefield. The correct use of ECM pods in the Falcon simulation will be explained later in this book.

FLYING FALCON

The Falcon is a unique aircraft to fly. The Falcon simulation captures much of the speed and power of flying the real jet and in doing so requires the "pilot" to know and practice air combat fundamentals. The rest of this book will teach the Falcon simulator pilot the requisite skills needed to fight in the hostile environment created in Falcon. This instruction parallels the actual courses taught to all new Falcon pilots, and also covers game-specific techniques. Armed with this knowledge, you will become a top-notch Falcon fighter pilot and a very dangerous adversary.

FALCON FUNDAMENTALS

3

"The air battle is not necessarily won at the time of the battle."

—Pappy Boyington
WWII American Ace

The mission of the fighter pilot is to fly and fight. Before you can fight however, you must first learn to fly. Fighter pilots training to fly the F-16 spend one year flying the T-37 and T-38 jet trainers, three months in Fighter Lead-In Training (again flying the T-38), and five months in F-16 Training. They are next sent to their squadrons for an additional two-to-three-month training course for Mission Qualification. After two years of training, students are combat-ready fighter pilots. Real combat better be another one to two years away, however, because at this point the "clue bag" of the new fighter pilot is still woefully empty. It will normally take another one to two years to get a grip on the fighter business, and acquire all of the skills needed to be effective in aerial combat.

Your training as a Falcon pilot started with a historical perspective. The next few chapters will expand this training by providing you with specifics of the Falcon simulation and air combat techniques. This training will make you a combat-ready fighter pilot in record time. This is possible, of course, because in the Falcon simulation you have only your pride to lose if you make a mistake.

AERODYNAMICS

Training starts with a very brief discussion of aerodynamics. Aerodynamics (or aero as pilots refer to it) is the engineering science that explains why aircraft fly. You do not need an in-depth understanding of aero to fly in the Falcon simulation, but you should know the forces that act on an aircraft in flight, and how they apply to Falcon performance.

The Forces Acting on the Jet

Thrust is a force that is directed out of the nose of the aircraft. This force, shown in Figure 3-1, is created when the engine pushes air out of the back

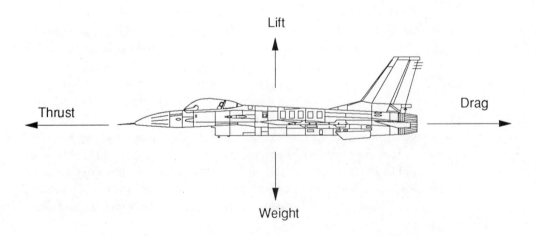

Figure 3-1.   Forces on the jet—thrust, lift, weight, and drag

of the jet. The jet engine sucks air into the intake, squeezes it in the compressor, mixes it with fuel, and ignites it in the combustion section. This air rapidly expands at ignition, and, when it is directed out of the back end of the jet, the pressure of air expansion propels the jet forward. You control this action with the throttle. The higher you push the throttle, the more thrust you get until you are at full Military power (MIL). *Military power* refers to normal, non-afterburning throttle settings. The *afterburner* (AB) is a section of the engine that can be selected by the pilot with the throttle. When selected, it dumps fuel into the aft end of the engine and ignites it, producing up to 40 percent more thrust (25000lbs in AB versus 15000lbs in MII). The AB gives you a large increase in thrust but it also burns up a lot of fuel (up to four times more than Military power).

Drag is the force acting opposite thrust. Figure 3-1 shows drag acting from the tail of the aircraft. Drag is produced anytime you push something (such as an airplane) through the air causing friction between the air and the aircraft body. The smaller the frontal area of your aircraft, the lower the drag, and the less thrust needed. Drag is also a function of design. A Corvette, for example, has a very *clean* aerodynamic design and low drag compared to a Jeep, which has a relatively *dirty* high-drag design. Aircraft are the same as cars in this respect. An F-16 has less drag due to air friction than an F-4 because of the F-16's smaller front and cleaner design. If you hang bombs on the F-16, however, you increase the frontal area and "dirty" up the aircraft, thereby increasing drag.

Lift is the force that counters the weight of the aircraft and enables it to fly. It is produced by the wings (and the fuselage in the F-16) and is directed forward the top of the jet, perpendicular to your flight path. Figure 3-1 shows the position of the lift vector.

Weight is also shown in Figure 3-1. *Weight* is the force on the aircraft that pulls it toward the earth. It is different from the other forces we have discussed because nothing the pilot does with his aircraft affects weight. If you dive straight down in your Falcon, weight will act in the same direction as thrust—straight down. Conversely, if you climb straight up, weight still pulls straight down towards the earth, opposing thrust.

Now that we have a basic understanding of why the pointy end of the jet goes through the sky first, it's time to discuss maneuvering.

Flight Mechanics

Airplanes can do only three basic things: roll, turn, and accelerate. The Red Baron's Fokker Tri-plane, United's Flight 205 to Chicago, and the Falcon simulation are all limited by these three basic maneuvers.

The *roll* is the first maneuver we will discuss. As you sit in the "cockpit" of the Falcon, picture a line that runs from the nose of the airplane, through the cockpit and out the tail of the jet. This line is called the *roll axis;* and *roll* is movement of the aircraft wings around this line.

Turn is movement of the nose that occurs as a result of rolling the aircraft. When you roll the wings of the aircraft and then stop the roll, you establish a *bank angle*. This angle is measured between the wings of your aircraft and the horizon. When you establish a bank with the wings, the aircraft turns in the direction of the low wing.

The rate at which the aircraft turns is determined in part by the Gs that the pilot pulls. The higher the Gs commanded by the pilot, the faster the aircraft turns (assuming a constant airspeed). The specifics of pulling Gs in Falcon will be covered later in this chapter. For now, you need to understand that during a level turn (assuming a constant altitude), there is a relationship between bank angle and Gs. If the pilot wants to execute a $2G$ level turn, for example, he must use 60 degrees of aircraft bank. A $6G$ turn requires 80 degrees of bank. Figure 3-2 shows aircraft Gs and the corresponding proper bank angle for a level turn. If you do not bank the aircraft at the proper bank angle for a particular G load, you will climb or descend. If you were at 60 degrees of bank and pulled $3G$s, the jet would climb. If you only pull $1.5G$s at 60 degrees of bank, the aircraft would descend.

Acceleration is simply speeding up or slowing down. This is accomplished in Falcon by increasing or decreasing power. Weight and drag also affect how fast you accelerate or decelerate.

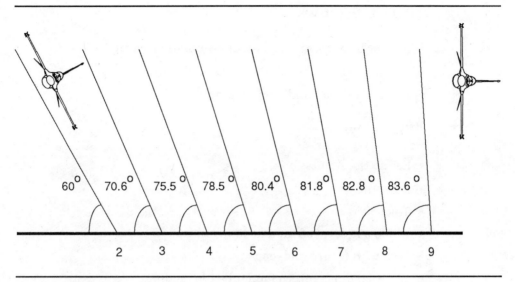

Figure 3-2.   *G*s and the corresponding bank angle

THE BRIEFING

Now that you have a few flight fundamentals under your belt, it's time to prepare for a training sortie in Falcon. The rest of this chapter will walk you through a training flight and will cover all the basic skills needed to fly in the Falcon simulation. Prior to takeoff on a fighter mission, you have a mission briefing. The purpose of the briefing is to ensure the flight members are all singing from the same sheet of music. The briefing covers the mission objectives and gives an overview of the tasks and maneuvers to be executed. The objectives and the overview are outlined here.

Mission Objectives

- Review basic cockpit layout and simulation set-up
- Learn how to fly aerobatics and combat turns
- Execute take-off and landing procedures

Mission Overview

- Set up the simulation
- Start the jet
- Take off
- Climb out, level off, and do low *G* turns
- Do a high *G* turn and loop
- Enter landing pattern for a full-stop landing

Figure 3-3 shows the profile that we will fly for this sortie.

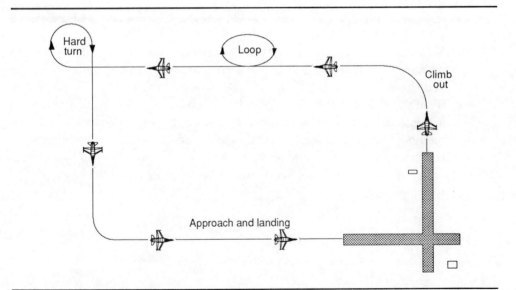

Figure 3-3.   Profile of the mission

Figure 3-4.   Falcon opening screen

PREFLIGHT

After briefing the mission, it's time for the preflight. The *preflight,* as the name implies, consists of checks and procedures that are performed by the pilot prior to takeoff. In the F-16, the pilot starts the preflight when he arrives at the jet. The first thing that he does is check the aircraft *forms.* All aircraft have a set of forms that show the flying record of the jet. These forms show information such as how much gas was put in the airplane, what systems are broken or degraded, and who flew the jet on the previous flight. After reviewing the forms, the pilot performs a walk around inspection. The *walk around* is an external inspection of the jet made just prior to "strapping in". In the Falcon simulation, our preflight will consist of setting up the Falcon, Duty Roster, Rank, and Armament screens. These screens perform various important preflight functions outlined in the next section.

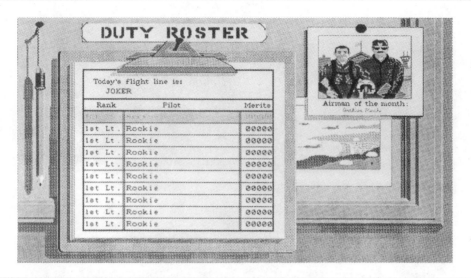

Figure 3-5. Duty Roster screen

The Falcon Screen

The first screen is the Falcon screen, shown in Figure 3-4. This screen has several selections listed across the top. These are File, Control, and Options. You move between these selections with the left and right arrow (← and →) keys, and within the categories under each selection with the up and down arrow (↑ and ↓) keys. Under File you can select Play or Quit. Under Control you select the method you will use to fly the Falcon, either keyboard or joystick. Throughout the book I will describe Falcon maneuvering using the keyboard for control. The Options selection lets you turn the simulation sound on or off and allows multiple computers to be hooked together. Since we will only discuss single-ship maneuvering, leave the number of players set to one.

The Duty Roster Screen

The next screen in Falcon is the Duty Roster. You get there from the Hardware screen by hitting the ENTER key. Figure 3-5 shows the duty

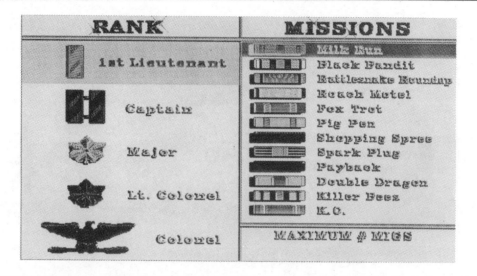

Figure 3-6.   Rank and Mission screen

roster where you type your name or tactical call sign. The duty roster contains a list of fighter pilots that are available for combat. If you have been greased (killed by the bad guys), captured, or court marshalled, you are obviously not able to fight and are removed from the duty roster. Use the up and down arrow (↑ and ↓) keys to select a spot on the duty roster, type your name and hit the ENTER key.

The Rank, Missions, and Number of MiGs Screen

The next screen is depicted in Figure 3-6 and contains Rank, Missions, and Maximum Number of MiGs. You move between these topics with the left and right arrow (← and →) keys, and you select the options with the up and down arrow (↑ and ↓) keys. Rank selects the level of difficulty. For this mission select Lieutenant. The Missions list provides a choice of profiles and objectives for your flight. These mission profiles require the pilot to

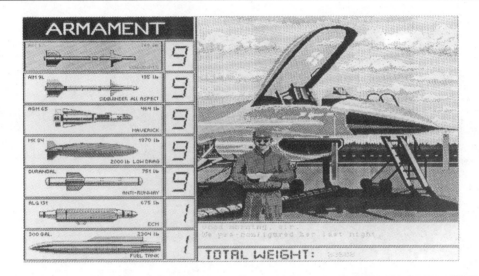

Figure 3-7. Armament screen

destroy specific targets in order to successfully accomplish the mission and receive a ribbon. For our training mission select Milk Run. For Maximum Number Of MiGs delete the MiGs appearing on the screen with the up and down arrow (↑ and ↓) keys and hit ENTER to move to the Armament screen.

The Armament Screen

The Armament screen, Figure 3-7, contains a list of pilot selectable external stores. Use the ↑ and ↓ keys to select the stores and the + and − keys to increase or decrease the store quantity. You can only increase or decrease store quantities in the ranks above Lieutenant. The Lieutenant rank automatically gives you an unlimited number of all possible weapons that the jet can carry. In the levels of the game above Lieutenant, the Sarge, to the right of the Armament list, will provide you feedback on the availability of your selections. Typically the Falcon pilot gets to the Armament screen with his fangs out and the smell of blood in his nostrils. This is good. As a fighter pilot your job is to stand between the "amber waves of grain" and the bankrupt ideology of the godless commies. The Sarge is there on the Armament screen to ensure that you don't trip on your fangs on the way to accomplishing this objective. He will prevent you from loading an asymmetrical (unbalanced) configuration, and he will warn you when the jet's weight prevents certain maneuvers (such as flying upside down). Hit the ENTER key when you are ready to climb into the jet.

If you need to change one of the previous screens any time during your preflight, hit the ESC key and select the Duty Roster from the menu. From there you can page back through the screens and make changes.

Clock Speed

A very important preflight item is the clock speed. Hitting the F8 key changes the CPU speed of the computer and will, in effect, control the passage of time during your mission. The first time you depress the F8 key you decrease the simulation speed. The second time you depress F8 you slow down the simulation by another order of magnitude. The third time you depress the F8 key you restore the simulation to the original value default speed. This key is used to make adjustments in the simulation for various computer CPU speeds and pilot proficiency. Slow the simulation down with this key if you have trouble keeping up with the jet.

THE MISSION

We are now strapped into the jet and ready to go. Before lighting the fire on this bird, let's review cockpit gauges and symbology. The first time I looked inside the cockpit of the F-16, I felt like a hog looking at a wrist-watch. After a few flights I became familiar with the cockpit layout and developed habits to effectively use all of the information displayed. The same will hold true for you in Falcon. Don't be overwhelmed by the volume of data that is presented to you in the cockpit.

The Cockpit

The cockpit is depicted in Figure 3-8 with the primary gauges and instruments labeled. If the picture on your computer screen does not look like Figure 3-8 after leaving the Armament screen, hit the 3 key to get to the center cockpit display. The 4 key gives you the left cockpit view and the 6 key gives you the right cockpit view. The 5 key provides the pilot with that all important six o'clock view out of the back of the jet.

Heads Up Display (HUD)

The most important part of the cockpit is the HUD. The HUD is used by the pilot for everything from weapons delivery to landing the aircraft. Figure 3-8 shows the HUD with the following important displays labeled.

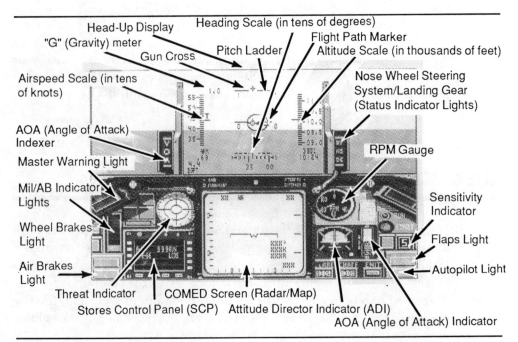

Figure 3-8. Falcon cockpit

Airspeed Scale   The Airspeed Scale is a sliding two-digit scale on the far-left side of the HUD that reads tens of knots. A small capital T is displayed over a horizontal line that marks the current airspeed. A T over a line at 40 would indicate the aircraft is flying 400 nautical miles per hour (knots).

Altitude Scale   The Altitude Scale is a sliding three-digit scale on the far- right hand side of the HUD that reads altitude in thousands of feet. A horizontal line in the center of the scale marks the aircraft altitude. If this line were on 10.5, the aircraft would be at 10,500 feet. In addition to this scale, an exact digital readout of aircraft altitude is displayed in the lower-right corner of the HUD.

Pitch Ladder   The Pitch Ladder is a series of horizontal lines that appear in the middle of the HUD. These lines represent tens of degrees and are labeled with a single positive or negative digit. The number 1, for example, means ten degrees.

Flight Path Marker   The Flight Path Marker is a circle with small wings and a small vertical tail that shows the direction your jet is moving through the sky relative to the horizon. The Flight Path Marker, when used in conjunction with the Pitch Ladder, gives the pilot his best cockpit reference for flying the jet. If you want to level off, for example, place the Flight Path Marker on the 0 Pitch Line and the jet will stay level. If you place the Flight Path Marker on the 1 Pitch Line, the jet will climb at ten degrees.

Heading Scale   The Heading Scale is a sliding horizontal scale at the bottom of the HUD that displays the direction of the aircraft over the ground (heading) in tens of degrees. A vertical line in the center of the scale marks the heading. If this vertical line were on 09, the aircraft heading would be 090 degrees. This scale shifts to the top of the HUD in the Air to Ground weapons modes to accommodate the HUD Air-to-Ground aiming symbology displayed in the lower portion of the HUD.

G Meter   A G Meter is located in the top-left corner of the HUD and it indicates current aircraft Gs to the nearest tenth. Since the simulation does not give you a "seat of the pants" reference for how hard you are turning, this *G* Meter is important. In a real F-16, when you start a hard turn, there is no doubt in your mind that you are at high *G*. The jet rudely slams you into the seat as the *G*s build, and your head weighs close to a hundred pounds during the turn. Nobody with a hundred-pound head wonders whether or not they are in a high *G* turn. In the simulation you can't feel the *G*s, so you must reference the *G* Meter in the HUD.

Gun Cross   The Gun Cross is a fixed reference at the top of the HUD that shows the departure line of your 20-mm cannon fire. The bullets fly out of the jet at the Gun Cross. We will discuss the significance of the Gun Cross as an aiming reference in the next chapter.

These are the primary displays presented in the HUD that will be used for this training flight. Other weapon-specific HUD displays will be addressed in later chapters.

The Center Cockpit Display

The center cockpit, shown in Figure 3-8, has several important displays and gauges that are not located in the HUD.

Radar/Map Display   This display is also known as the COMED Screen and shows the Falcon radar or a map of the area with your aircraft position displayed as a flashing square. You can toggle between radar and map by hitting the **C** key.

Stores Control Panel (SCP)   This is located to the left of the radar, and it displays the current weapon modes selected.

Threat Indicator   This is located above the SCP and it displays the presence of MiGs or enemy Surface-to-Air Missiles (SAMs), and gives the pilot the relative azimuth of the threat by displaying a square on the screen. We will cover the Threat Indicator in more detail in Chapter 5.

Attitude Director Indicator (ADI)   This circular gauge, located to the right of the radar screen, shows the aircraft climb angle (pitch) and bank angle relative to the horizon. The top of the ADI is light colored to represent the sky, and the bottom is dark to represent the earth. This display acts like the Flight Path Marker and the Pitch Lines in the HUD and gives the pilot an indication of aircraft pitch and bank.

RPM Gauge   This is located directly above the ADI and gives the pilot an indication of the thrust setting (or throttle position) in percent. At 60 percent power on the RPM Gauge, the Falcon is at idle power, and producing zero thrust. At 100 percent on the RPM Gauge, the Falcon is at full Military power.

MIL/AB Indicator Lights   These are located on the far-left side of the cockpit, and show whether the engine is in MIL or AB. If the afterburner has been selected, "AB" appears and the display shows the five stages of AB with a series of vertically stacked lights. If the engine is in MIL, "MIL" is displayed.

     Several other indicator lights are also present in the cockpit. These lights include the Wheel Brake Light, the Air Brake Light, the Flaps Light, the Autopilot Light, the Start Light, and the Nose Gear Steering/Landing Gear Indicator Lights. These indicator lights are labeled in Figure 3-8 and are either on or off depending on the status of the mode they represent. For example, when the air brakes are extended, the Air Brake Light is illuminated.

The Left Cockpit Display

The important gauges on the left cockpit view are depicted in Figure 3-9. You get to this screen by hitting the 4 key. The displays on this screen include the following:

Back Up Airspeed Indicator   The Back Up Airspeed Indicator is located to the far right of the screen and displays airspeed in tens of knots. This gauge is used if your HUD fails. In the simulation, just as in the real F-16, you may lose critical systems such as the HUD due to battle damage or routine failure.

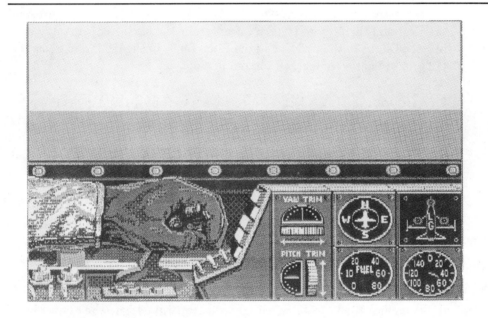

Figure 3-9. Left cockpit display

Landing Gear (LG) Indicator   The Landing Gear Indicator is located above the Back Up Airspeed Indicator and shows the status of all three landing gear.

Fuel Gauge   The Fuel Gauge is located to the left of the Back Up Airspeed Indicator and shows fuel remaining in hundreds of pounds. The word "Fuel" displayed in the HUD means you are probably close to running dry so think about getting back to the field. Any jet with an afterburner is always short on gas. Monitor this gauge continually throughout the flight or you may end up a glider pilot in a war where glider pilots have a very short life span.

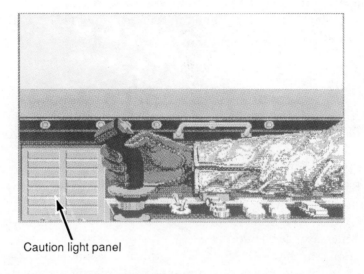

Caution light panel

Figure 3-10.   Right cockpit display

Back Up Heading Indicator   The Back Up Heading Indicator is located above the Fuel Gauge and displays the aircraft heading. This gauge is a backup to the HUD heading scale.

The Right Cockpit Display

This screen, shown in Figure 3-10, contains the Caution Light Panel. You get to the right cockpit display by hitting the 6 key. When you get a flashing Master Caution Light in the front cockpit screen, the damaged system will be illuminated on this panel. For example, if your flaps are damaged, you will get a Master Caution Light in the front cockpit and an illuminated Flaps Light on the Caution Light Panel. Damaged systems normally occur in Falcon due to enemy action. When the bad guys shoot missiles at you, which blow up in your general vicinity, you may end up with a bent (damaged) airplane. When damage to your jet occurs, you will normally get a Master Caution Light and can reference the Caution Light Panel to find the affected system.

Engine Start

The time has finally come to get some air between your rear end and Mother Earth (all simulated of course). The first thing to do is start the engine.

When you first "enter" the cockpit and hit the + key, you engage the Jet Fuel Starter (JFS), which in turn starts the engine. Hitting the + key initiates the following sequence: a high-pitched whine occurs as the JFS engages, the JFS Start Light depicted in Figure 3-8 illuminates, and the RPM increases to 60 percent.

Sometimes the JFS fails. When this occurs the JFS Start Light will go out and the RPM will fall to zero percent. All you have to do when the start fails is try the start again.

During the start sequence, the Wheel Brakes Light, "WL BRK", should be illuminated to indicate that the wheel brakes are engaged. The jet will not move when this light is on.

The Throttle

Before takeoff, we need to understand how to use the throttle and the stick to maneuver the jet. Throttle position in Falcon is controlled by the + and - keys on the keyboard. Hitting the + key advances the power, and hitting the - key retards power. You can monitor the thrust you are producing in Falcon by monitoring the RPM Gauge. The RPM Gauge is shown in Figure 3-8. The reading on the RPM Gauge is directly proportional to airspeed in the Lieutenant level we have selected. For example, if you advance the power to 80 percent power on the RPM Gauge, the jet will fly at about 450 knots. If you pull the power back to 60 percent, you are commanding zero thrust so the jet will slow rapidly, stall, and crash. The maximum RPM reading is 100 percent, and this setting is full Military power.

Maximum thrust is obtained by using the afterburner. The / key toggles the engine in and out of AB. You can hit this key at any RPM level; the engine will accelerate to 100 percent power and the AB will light. Once you have engaged the afterburner with the / key there are five stages or levels of AB that are controlled by the < and > keys.

You gain an additional stage of AB with each hit of the < key. You can also just hold this key down until all stages of AB are engaged. You lose an AB stage each time you press the > key, or by holding it down steadily, you can return to the first stage.

You can leave AB entirely with the / key. Hitting the / key disengages the AB completely and returns the engine to 100 percent MIL power. Hitting the / key a second time will toggle you back into AB. You can monitor the stage and status of the AB (on or off) by referencing the AB/MIL lights shown in Figure 3-8.

The throttle, RPM Gauge, and the MIL/AB indicators are very important in Falcon. *The single biggest mistake in the Falcon simulation is airspeed control.* There is a tendency to fully accelerate and just race around the combat area with your hair on fire. This may be fun but it will not win you many fights. You must learn to constantly adjust the throttle to fly at the correct airspeed for the tactical situation. More on this later.

The Stick

You control aircraft movement in Falcon with the "stick". The F-16 is the only operational fighter with a side stick controller. Old-fashioned jets (like the F-15) have control sticks located between the pilot's legs. The F-16 has a *force feel,* side stick located on the right side of the cockpit that only moves about 1/8 of an inch in response to pilot input. The side stick senses pressure and moves the flight controls in response to this pressure. By contrast, the flight controls in conventional aircraft move in response to the physical movement of the control stick. In Falcon you have the option of using the keyboard or a joystick to replicate the function of the F-16 stick. In our discussion we will explain movement of the stick and control of the Falcon via the keyboard controls as shown in Figure 3-11. The arrows on the numeric key pad move the stick in the indicated direction. For example, to pull back on the stick, hit the ↓ arrow. This will apply

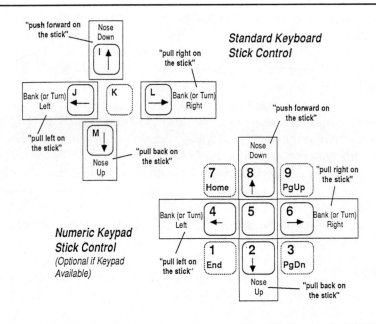

Figure 3-11. Keyboard controls

backward stick pressure and increasing G force as long as you hold the key down. When you release a key, the stick automatically centers and you will no longer be commanding stick pressure.

The rest of the keyboard controls work in the same way as the ↓ arrow. The stick movement commanded along with the corresponding G force and aircraft nose movement are explained here:

The ↓ key   This commands back stick pressure and higher Gs, and moves the aircraft's nose up.

The ↑ key   This commands forward stick pressure and lower Gs, and moves the aircraft's nose down.

The → key   This commands right stick movement and right roll/bank of the aircraft wings.

The ← key   This commands left stick movement and left roll/bank of the aircraft wings.

We will address actual aircraft maneuvers with these keys once you are airborne.

Takeoff

Takeoff is the most dangerous non-combat phase of any fighter sortie. The reason for this is three-fold: during takeoff the jet is heavy, slow, and close to the ground, which gives you little margin for error in aircraft control. The F-16 has a big motor pushing it which makes takeoffs relatively easy and safe. Even so, take special care to execute proper take-off procedures in the Falcon simulation to ensure you don't give the enemy a victory without any shots being fired.

We are lined up on Runway 36 and ready for takeoff. The engine is running, and the RPM Gauge is indicating 60 percent. Depress the + key to advance the power to 80 percent. At 80 percent, release the + key and hit the **W** key to release the wheel brakes. *Do not advance the power past 80 percent without releasing the wheel brakes or damage to the aircraft may occur.* After releasing the wheel brakes, continue advancing the power to 100 percent. The Airspeed Scale in the HUD will start to move, and you will notice the jet rolling down the runway. When the airspeed reaches 150 knots (15 in the HUD), hit the ↓ key on the keyboard to apply back stick pressure and rotate the Flight Path Marker to ten degrees up on the Pitch Lines in the HUD (ten degrees is the line with a 1 beside it). Your HUD should look the same as Figure 3-12.

Once you note the altitude increasing on the left scale of the HUD, raise the landing gear by hitting the **G** key on the keyboard. Hit the **4** key to insure that the gear lights are out in the Landing Gear Indicator display on the left cockpit screen. After checking the gear, hit the **3** key to return to the front cockpit display.

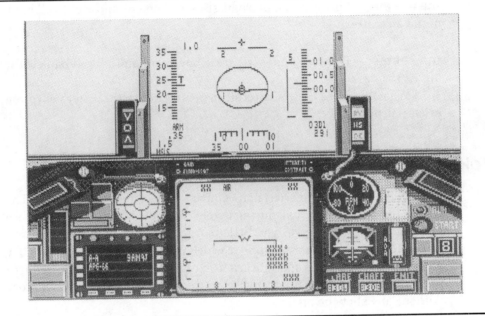

Figure 3-12. 10-degree climb

Climb Out and Cruise

Keep the jet climbing at ten degrees nose up, and retard the power to 80 percent on the RPM Gauge by hitting the - key. The airspeed will stabilize at about 450 knots. Move the throttle up and down and note the changing RPM and the corresponding change in airspeed. At the Lieutenant level the only thing that influences airspeed is throttle position. When the altitude approaches 10,000 feet (10.0 on the HUD Altitude Scale) level off by pushing the nose down with the ↑ key. Keep hitting this key until the Flight Path Marker is on the 0 Pitch Line in the HUD.

Now that you are leveled off, hit the **P** key to pause/freeze the simulation. Hitting the **P** key will toggle the simulation in and out of the pause mode. When engaged, the pause will not allow any keyboard input and will freeze the jet in midair.

Falcon Maneuvering

Before we fly any further, let's talk about some fundamental aircraft maneuvering. Maneuvering the jet is nothing more than changing your direction using the "stick". The following list describes basic flight maneuvers and the necessary stick input. Toggle the simulation in and out of the pause mode to read the text and execute the following maneuvers:

Roll/Bank   To roll the wings of the aircraft, depress either the → or the ← key, depending on the desired direction of roll. If you hit and release the key the wings will establish a bank angle and stop. If you keep the key depressed, you will continue the roll until you release the key.

Climb   To climb in Falcon, first make sure the wings are level with the horizon; roll if necessary to get the wings level. Next hit the ↓ key once. The nose of the aircraft will rise in relation to the horizon. The Flight Path Marker in the HUD will also rise in relation to the Pitch Lines. If you hold this key down, the nose of the jet will continue to climb.

Descend   To descend, depress the ↑ key. Again, by holding the key down you will continue to apply nose down stick pressure.

Low G Turns   These are turns of less than three Gs. These types of turns are used to change aircraft direction when only a small heading change is required or when you do not want to rapidly move the nose. To execute a low G turn, depress the → key and roll the aircraft into a right bank angle of 30-60 degrees. The greater the bank angle, the faster you will turn, but do not let the bank angle exceed 60 degrees. You can check the bank angle by looking at the ADI in the cockpit.

During the turn, you may need to depress the ↑ or the ↓ key momentarily to keep the Flight Path Marker on 0 Pitch Line and the aircraft level.

You will notice the heading indicator in the HUD gradually changing headings. Keep turning to the right and when you get to 260 degrees (26 on the heading indicator), roll out of the turn using the ← key. By the time you get the wings level, the aircraft should be on a heading of 27 degrees. When you have an exact heading you wish to roll out on (during landing for example), you must start your roll out prior to getting to the desired heading or you will overshoot.

High *G* Turns

The ability to execute *high G turns,* and move the nose of the aircraft rapidly, separates the fighters from the targets. We will now execute a high *G turn.*

In the first section of this chapter we discussed the relationship of bank angles to *G*s during a level turn. This relationship is depicted in Figure 3-2. There are two major differences between executing a high and low *G* turn in Falcon. In the *high G turn* you use a steeper bank angle and greater back stick pressure. In a *low G turn* you just roll the wings to set a shallow bank angle (less than 60 degrees), and the nose of the jet slowly moves in the direction of the low wing with no back stick pressure required. The following steps are used to perform a high *G* turn.

1. Roll the jet into a 75-85 degrees of right bank using the → key.

2. After establishing the bank angle, apply back stick pressure by hitting the ↓ key. Keep hitting the key to establish five to six *G*s on the HUD *G Meter.*

3. You will invariably climb or descend if you do not have the perfect bank angle established. If this happens you will notice the Flight Path Marker moving off the 0 Pitch Line in the HUD. To remedy the situation, stop the back stick pressure by depressing the ↓ key and adjust the bank angle of the jet right (→ key) or left (← key) depending on whether you are climbing or descending.

   • If you were climbing during the turn, steepen up the bank with the → key and then reapply back stick pressure with the ↓ key and get back to five to six *G*s.

   • If you were descending during your 5-6 *G* turn, shallow out the bank angle by rolling the wings left with the ← key then reapply back pressure with the ↓ key and go back to five to six *G*s.

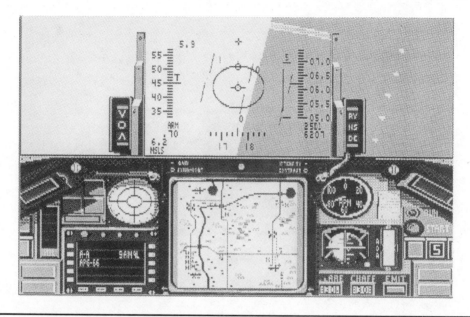

Figure 3-13. High *G* turn

4. Keep the turn coming and roll out your original heading of 270 degrees (27 on the HUD Heading Indicator). Remember to lead the roll out or you will overshoot the 270 heading.

A high *G* level turn requires a steep bank angle that increases as the Gs increase. Increased Gs generally cause the jet to turn tighter and faster. It is important that you can execute a hard turn so keep practicing this maneuver until you can do a level five to six *G* turn. Figure 3-13 shows a high *G* turn.

Speed Brake Drill

Now that you are back on a heading of 270 degrees, hit the **C** key to call up the Map Display. You will recall that the **C** key toggles the radar screen

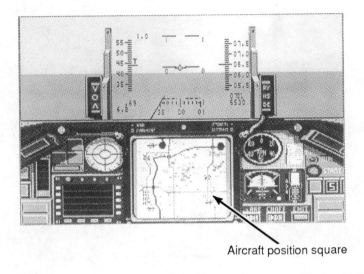

Aircraft position square

Figure 3-14. Map display after takeoff

between the radar and Map Display. Once you have entered the map mode, note the flashing square on the display. This is your position in the Falcon world. Figure 3-14 shows the Map Display and an aircraft position on the map. The top of the map is always north, regardless of your aircraft heading. You will notice as you fly heading west (270 degrees) that the flashing black square will move over the map on the same heading.

Next depress the **B** key to deploy the speed brakes. The speed brakes, also called "the boards", are high-drag devices designed to slow the jet down. The boards are used frequently in air-to- air combat to kill off excess *smash* (overtaking airspeed) when attacking an enemy aircraft. They are also used in routine non-combat flying to slow the jet down without using the throttle. When you put the boards out in Falcon, notice the Brake Light in the cockpit and the airspeed deceleration on the Airspeed Indicator. Hit the **B** key to retract the speed brakes, and the airspeed will accelerate back to your original speed.

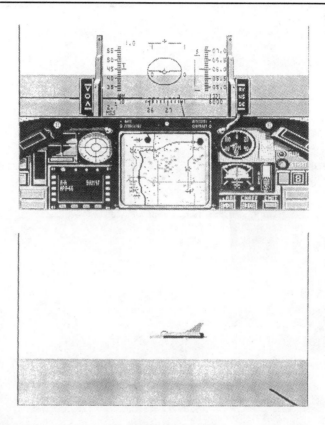

Figure 3-15.   Loop starting position

Performing a Loop

Doing a loop in the Falcon is really a simple maneuver that requires some easy stick and throttle input. The following steps describes the procedures for executing a loop:

1. Set the power at 80 percent to establish airspeed at 400-450 knots.

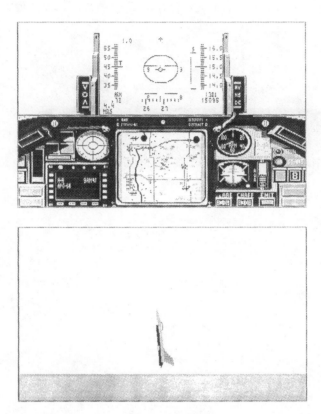

Figure 3-16. Climbing straight up in a loop

2. Next, descend to 6,000 feet by depressing the ↑ key. Establish the
    Flight Path Marker on the -1 line in the HUD (this equates to ten
    degrees of dive). When you get to about 6,500 feet (6.5 on the HUD
    altitude scale), start pulling the Flight Path Marker up to the 0
    Pitch Line in the HUD using the ↓ key. (*Note:* There is nothing
    really significant about starting the loop at 6,000 feet other than
    I wanted to run through another altitude change example.) We
    are now ready for the loop. Figure 3-15 shows the correct position
    prior to commencing the loop.

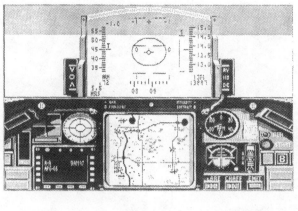

Figure 3-17.   Inverted position in a loop

3. Start applying back stick pressure with the ↓ key, bringing the nose of the jet straight up and over the top. Figure 3-16 shows the HUD and an outside view of the jet climbing straight up. Notice the position of the Flight Path Marker. *Do not pause in this position.* Keep the ↓ key depressed and keep the nose moving. Figure 3-17 shows the aircraft in an inverted position on the top of the loop. Notice the horizon at the top of the HUD. Figure 3-18 shows the aircraft heading straight down the back side of the loop.

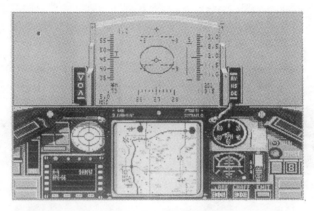

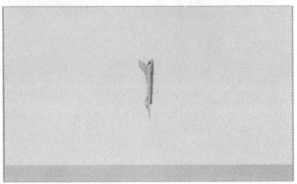

Figure 3-18. Backside of loop

4. Keep applying back stick pressure until the Flight Path Marker gets ten degrees nose down in the HUD (the -1 pitch line). At this point release back stick pressure by releasing the ↓ key. You should roll out with the same HUD view as shown in Figure 3-15; the Flight Path Marker in the HUD should be on the 0 degree Pitch Line. Practice doing loops to get the feel of maneuvering the jet vertically. After you are comfortable doing loops, move on to the next section.

Landing the Falcon

Landing is second only to takeoff as the most dangerous non- combat phase of flight. The reason it is second is that the jet is not as heavy landing as it is taking off. I spent about three years teaching pilots to land the F-16 and in that time I have seen the landing runway from a number of interesting perspectives.

One day I was in the bar after the flying was over swapping "war" stories with a buddy of mine, Slick. Slick started the conversation by telling me that he had seen a very interesting spectacle while out at "mobile". (*Mobile* is a small elevated glass building located at the end of the runway where instructors observe student landings.) Slick was sitting out there reading magazines and watching airplanes land when he saw an F-16 coming in to land, steep on glide path, about two miles out on final approach. This interested him so he put down his copy of *Readers' Digest,* and focused his attention on what appeared to be a plumber trying to land an F-16. As the jet approached he saw it was a two-seat B model. This meant there was an IP (instructor pilot) in the "pit" (back seat) of the jet so he relaxed a little. As it got closer, though, the landing went from bad to worse, and the jet started dropping like a rock toward the runway. A hundred feet above the runway, the pilot went to full AB to arrest his descent but it didn't help. Slick grabbed the radio to tell the pilot to go around but it was too late. The jet hit like a ton of bricks and bounced in the air, banked 90 degrees at about 50 feet off the runway, and lumbered back into the sky. Slick said he was so stunned and scared, he never even made a radio call.

During this tale I just kind of nodded my head, and acted interested and surprised. When he was finished with the story I just drank down my whiskey, mumbled something about being glad I wasn't in mobile, and headed out the door. Unfortunately I had an even better view of the whole thing than Slick did because I was the IP in the pit during that landing. I let the student stray a little too far out of safe landing parameters and when I finally took control of the airplane the only thing that stood between our sorry behinds and a crash landing was God and that big Pratt and Whitney engine. I never did tell Slick that I was the IP in the back seat of that jet, but I think he already knew. The lesson I learned that day was:

don't ever get complacent in the landing pattern. Hit your parameters or go around and try it again. This lesson also holds true in the simulation.

The ultimate objective in Falcon air combat is to make the number of successful landings match the number of takeoffs. The next section will help you master the difficult art of landing the Falcon. It is a real shame to shoot down the MiGs, destroy the target, and survive the mission, only to get morted (killed) trying to put the airplane back on the runway.

There is an infinite number of landing techniques possible in the simulation, and the following is only one of them. If you do not already have your own technique for landing the jet, these steps will help you put the Falcon safely on the runway. Use the P key frequently during the landing sequence to make sure you are staying up with the jet.

1. Check your position on the map and ensure the jet is Northwest of the field in the approximate position depicted by the square in Figure 3-19. You have several options if the jet is not in this position. The first is to turn the aircraft in the direction of the area shown in Figure 3-19. Once you arrive at the proper location, turn to 270 degrees and continue on to step two. The other option is to hit the ESC key and return to the Duty Roster. From here, start the mission over again. This time take off and, after you raise the gear, pull the power back to 70 percent and level off at 3,000 feet. Fly north (00 degrees in the HUD) until you get to a major east/west road as shown in Figure 3-19. Approaching the road, turn to a heading of 270 degrees, and fly until you get to the location shown in Figure 3-19. Once in this position, go to step two.

2. The jet should be heading 270 degrees with the map mode selected. Start a low *G* left turn to enter the landing pattern by hitting the ← key. Roll out on a heading of 180 degrees. Next comes the landing pattern.

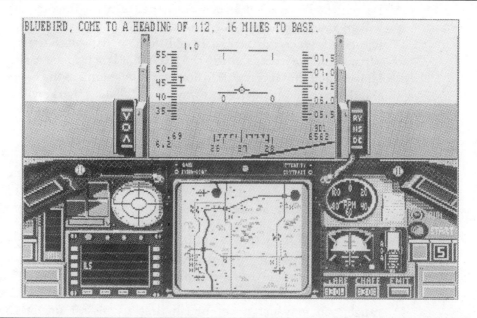

Figure 3-19. Map display of landing position

3. Hit the F7 function key to call up the Instrument Landing System (ILS). The letters "ILS" will appear on the SCP to confirm you are in the landing mode. With ILS displayed on the SCP, the computer will issue you headings, and dashed horizontal and vertical bars will appear in the HUD. More on this later.

4. Cut the power back to 70 percent on the RPM Gauge. This will stabilize your airspeed at 200 knots.

5. Descend and level off at 3,000 feet. In the ILS mode the computer will give you headings to turn to and distances to the field at the top of the front cockpit screen. In addition, you will get the dashed vertical and horizontal bars in the HUD that I mentioned earlier. I have found that it is better to disregard these bars in the Falcon simulation and line up the runway using the directions given by the computer, the Map display, and your Heading Indicator in the HUD.

6. Read the computer generated heading directions at the top of the screen. Disregard all of these headings until you get a call to come to a heading of 110-120 degrees. When you get a call that is within this range, start a left turn to roll out on the computer-directed heading. (A word of caution about distance to the field. It is important not to turn toward the field until you are at least 15 miles away. The computer generated calls in the ILS mode will give you the range of the Falcon to the runway along with heading information. If you start a turn toward the field inside of a 15-mile range, you may not have enough time to get set up for the landing.)

7. The computer will keep telling you the heading to the field. Follow these headings. The landing runway is 09, which means your heading on final will be 090 degrees (09 on the HUD Heading Scale.) If you are more than ten degrees off this heading, it is not a major problem. Just anticipate making a turn to line up with the runway once you see the field.

8. When you are ten miles from the field descend to 2,000 feet.

9. During the descent at ten miles, extend the Landing Gear by hitting the **G** key. Confirm the gear are down by depressing the **4** key and checking for gear lights in the Landing Gear Indicator.

10. Extend the flaps by hitting the **F** key. The Flaps light in the front cockpit screen will illuminate when the flaps are down.

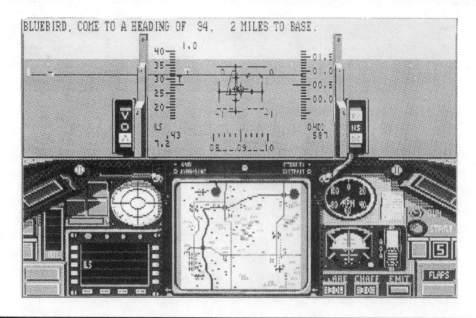

Figure 3-20. Landing aircraft—two miles from the runway

11. When you get about four miles from the field start a gentle descent by putting the Flight Path Marker slightly below the 0 Pitch Line in the HUD. The exact altitude readout in the bottom-right corner of the HUD should be monitored so as not to go below 1,000 feet until you have the runway in sight.

12. Adjust the RPM to slow down to between 150-200 knots. As you gain proficiency, strive to land at 150 knots. This will make stopping the jet easier (and it looks more stylish to land slowly).

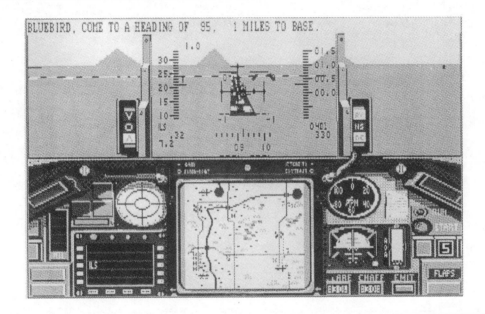

Figure 3-21. Landing aircraft—one mile from the runway

13. Keep following the headings of the computer and make small bank angle corrections to get on the correct heading.

14. When you have the field in sight, place the Flight Path Marker about one quarter of the way down the runway and keep coming down. The closer you get to landing, the smaller the pitch and bank corrections you need to make. Figure 3-20 shows the Falcon two miles from the field with the runway in sight. Note the altitude of 587 feet.

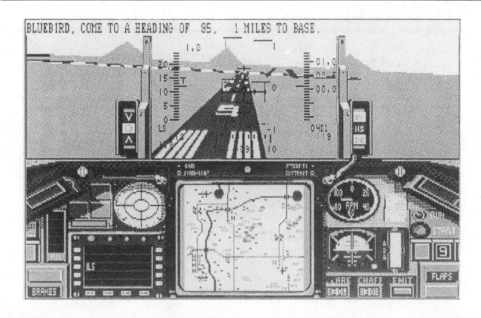

Figure 3-22. Landing aircraft—approaching the runway

15. Figure 3-21 is the same landing sequence with the jet one mile from the field. The altitude is now 330 feet and the Flight Path Marker is three to four degrees below the 0 Pitch Line in the HUD, one quarter of the way down the runway. When the landing picture looks like Figure 3-22, retard the throttle to idle and extend the Speed brakes (hit the **B** key). In this picture the jet is at 119 feet and lined up for landing.

16. At touchdown the nose will drop and the altitude will read zero. When this occurs, apply the Wheel Brakes (with the **W** key) and steer toward the center of the runway using normal aircraft controls.

MISSION DEBRIEFING

Well, nobody said it would be easy. If you want to do something easy, get up from the computer, and go back to holding hands with sweet Marie. It will definitely take you a few times in the landing circuit before you can safely bring this bird to roost.

This training sortie reviewed the basics of flying the jet. Once you get a general idea on how to fly, it's time to start the fighting. In the next chapter we will discuss weapons. Armed with weapons we will seek out and engage the enemy.

Air Combat Weapons

4

*"Mamas don't let your babies grow up to fly
fighters, don't let 'em shoot missiles and drop
bombs on trucks, make 'em be doctors and
lawyers and such..."*

—Fight Pilot adaptation of
a famous Willie Nelson song

The scenario was standard for a Battlefield Air Interdiction mission. An enemy tank division was moving up to reinforce a combined arms division that was locked in combat with U.S. forces along the forward line of troops (FLOT). In addition to the standard Surface to Air Missile (SAM) threat, the enemy had air cover over the advancing Division. Our job was to attack the forward elements of this tank division with Maverick missiles. The "real" target for the mission was a collection of burned-out tank hulks to the north of Nellis Air Force Base. The "real" threat for the mission was two Navy Aggressor A-4s, simulating MiGs. I was flying with a guy named Skip on a fun-filled, action-packed Weapons School sortie. (The Weapons School is a very demanding four-month course in F-16 Weapons and Tactics, which I will describe in more detail throughout the book.)

On this sortie, Skip and I were both carrying live Maverick missiles. My recent poor performance on an earlier live weapons mission gave me extra incentive to get that coveted big *E* on this ride. The big *E* was a perverse Weapons School term. When you landed from a Weapons School ride, the Instructor at the Duty Desk in the Squadron filled out a form. On this form you signed in, filled out your flight time, and noted whether or not the sortie was "effective". An effective sortie meant you passed the ride and got an *E* on the form; a non-effective sortie or *NE* meant you flunked. When you got back from a Weapons School mission, you always nonchalantly sauntered over to the Duty Desk before the debrief to check the sign-in form for the big *E*. There were a few times when you definitely knew you had passed or failed the ride but most of the time it was a toss-up.

The mission was going smoothly as we approached the tank hulks. I had two bandits on my radar in trail formation, about five miles from the target area. The A-4 does not have air-to-air radar so these two Navy aggressors were groping around blind trying to find us. Using our radar "grip," we easily swung around to their six o'clock unobserved and attacked them with Aim-9Ls (simulated of course). After quickly "killing" both of them, we continued our attack on the tanks. The plan was for me to attack the farthest tank in the column and for Skip to attack the closest one. I called up the Maverick missile and started my attack from about three miles out.

The air-to-ground modes in the F-16 can be accessed by the pilot with the Dogfight/Missile Override thumb switch. This switch is located on the throttle and has three positions: forward, aft, and center. The forward and aft detents are air-to-air weapons modes. The center detent can be programmed by the pilot to call up air-to-ground weapons. On this ride I had the Maverick missile programmed to come up when I selected the center position on the Dogfight/Override switch.

Upon entering the Maverick mode the radar screen is transformed into a TV picture that shows a view from the Maverick missile. This TV picture has an Aiming Cross located in the center that can be controlled by the pilot. To execute an attack, you point the Aiming Cross in the HUD at the target and look down at the TV picture to lock-on.

You lock-on to the target by slewing (or turning) the Aiming Cross located in the radar scope (now a TV picture) with the Cursor/Enable button, which is also located on the throttle. You use this button to move the Aiming Cross over the target and lock-on. Once you lock-on, the Cross will stabilize on the target and you can fire the missile. What makes this type of attack sporting is the ground rushing up at you at about 800 feet per second while you are trying to look into the radar and lock-on to the target. Of course, "if you're afraid / you'll have to overlook it / because you knew the job / was dangerous when you took it." These words to the old Super Chicken cartoon are a good thing to keep in mind during most Maverick attacks in the F-16.

I picked up the tank column and rolled in on the end tank in the column. The Maverick locked-on to the tank, and I quickly checked the lock and hit the "pickle" button. The plane shuddered slightly as the Maverick rocket motor ignited and the missile left the launch rail. The jet was instantly covered in white smoke as 500 pounds of supersonic metal headed for the target. I immediately broke left to clear my six o'clock and gain sight of my wingman, and I gained a visual on Skip just as he fired his missile. We quickly got back in formation, and on the way out of the target area we again picked up the aggressors on radar. We were playing "30-second kill removal" so these guys had "come back to life" and were looking for us. This was a mistake. We had a good radar grip at 10 miles and for the second time attacked them unobserved. After killing both of them again, we exited the area and headed back toward home. I figured I was a shoo-in for the big *E*.

After landing, we went back into the squadron to sign in and debrief, and, sure enough, when I checked the sign-in forms, there it was—the big *E*. It may have only been black ink written on paper, but it appeared to glimmer like a jewel.

During the debrief we reviewed the aircraft VCR tape to check our missile shots. The F-16 has a VCR that can film the HUD or the radar scope. The pilot selects which one he wishes to record and turns the camera on. The Maverick missile gives you a TV picture presented in the radar scope of what the seeker head of the missile is seeing. You can record this picture and review it after you land.

I put my tape in the VCR and watched my attack. I saw the tank come into view and saw my maverick lock-on to it. The lock-on was very unstable, which I had not noticed during the flight. In a good Maverick lock-on the Aiming Cross is solid and stable on the target. In a bad lock the Aiming Cross is jittery and moves in relation to the target. As the tape continued I was dumbfounded when the Maverick Aiming Cross jumped from the tank I was aiming at to a nearby bush. Just a split second after this happened the screen went blank, indicating that the missile had been fired. I looked over at Skip, smiled feebly, and said, "whoops." I never noticed that the missile had transferred lock to the bush, and I didn't watch the missile hit the ground because I was breaking to clear my six o'clock.

Skip didn't look too concerned but he did say, "Maybe I didn't make the objective of this flight clear enough in the briefing. We were out there to kill enemy tanks, not shrubbery." He found this comment to be very funny, and was so amused by the whole thing that he invited the entire squadron to come into the debriefing room to watch me kill the bush. "Well, there goes the big *E,* I thought. The "peanut gallery" all piled into the room and got a good laugh at my expense. When they finally cleared out of the briefing room and we finished the debrief, I ended up passing the ride. (Well, I did lead a mission where we killed four "MiGs" and were one out of two for Maverick hits.) Skip said my performance was "indeed average." I think I must have caught him in an exceptionally charitable mood that day and was thankful to escape with the big *E,* no matter how average my flight.

THE FALCON AIR WAR

The Maverick missile I fired that day was designed to solve specific tactical problems. The modern battle tank is a tough target to kill. The Maverick is not perfect, but it does provide the F-16 with an effective tank-killing weapon.

The Maverick, like a number of other weapons carried by today's fighters, is highly accurate and lethal, but difficult to use and relatively expensive. Because of the expense, these weapons, however effective, are limited in quantity. The F-16 overcomes the potential problem of running out of these "silver bullet" weapons by having a *smart* weapon delivery system. A smart delivery system ties together the aircraft radar, navigation aids, and cockpit displays to give the jet the capability to deliver *dumb* iron bombs with great accuracy (as in the Israeli raid on Osirak). The air-to-ground munitions carried by the F-16 are a balance of smart and dumb weaponry.

Survivability

Today's fighter aircraft must be able to survive in the air battle, and having a lethal weapon system is a large part of survivability. Modern combat is fought with accurate and deadly firepower. Use of the electromagnetic spectrum for sensors and weapon guidance has produced a battlefield featuring *bull's-eye weapons*. Single targets are now engaged and destroyed with single, highly accurate weapons, rather than volleys of inaccurate projectiles. In this environment, the ability to minimize your exposure to the threat and to engage targets with accurate and lethal weapons is essential. In fighters, you minimize your exposure to threat systems by using speed, stand-off weapons (silver bullets), low radar, IR, and visual profiles. This is part of the *survival* side of the air battle equation. Another part of survival is the use of countermeasures such as electronic jamming, chaff, and flares to negate enemy threat systems.

Lethality

The other side of the air battle equation is the *lethality* of your own weapons against the enemy. Here you must have an on-board weapons suite capable of delivering accurate, destructive firepower. Modern fighters such as the F-16 are *weapon systems*. These aircraft contain avionics and weapons that, together with the aircraft's flying characteristics, make up the weapons system's capability. The F-16 is a lethal weapon system that can deliver both smart and dumb munitions with accuracy.

FALCON AIR-TO-AIR WEAPONS

The Falcon simulation recreates the F-16 weapon system and the air combat environment in which it operates. In the simulation, the Falcon can be armed with a variety of weapons. This chapter will teach you the characteristics of these weapons, and their associated HUD symbology, but will not cover employment techniques.

The Gun

There are times in a fight when things get "up close and personal." In most air-to-air combat engagements, the adversaries are thousands of feet

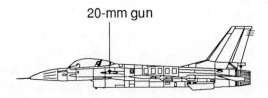

Figure 4-1.   F-16 M61 20-mm gun

apart, fighting with missiles. If no one gets morted quickly, these engagements usually get smaller and tighter until the opponents are virtually fighting in a "phone booth". When this occurs your missiles are useless. Missiles can be compared to the lance carried by a knight in a joust. You need a certain distance between the lancer and the lancee in order for this weapon to work. You definitely can't use it when you and your adversary are duking it out in a phone booth.

When you are hand fighting in close quarters, the best weapon is a knife. The F-16's air combat "knife," is the 20-mm cannon. When you are so close to the bandit that you can read his tail number, it's time to draw your M61. The gun in the F-16 is the M61-A1 Vulcan 20-mm cannon. The M61 is a six-barreled Gatling gun that fires 20-mm projectiles out to an effective range of 2,000 feet. The F-16 carries 510 rounds of 20-mm ammunition and fires at a rate of 100 rounds per second. It is primarily an air-to-air weapon but can be used in the air-to-ground role in emergencies.

The gun is located on the left side of the fuselage above the left strake. Figure 4-1 shows the location of the M61 on the F-16. The M61 in the Falcon simulation is similar in many respects to the gun in the F-16. The major differences are range and rounds on board. In Falcon, the jet carries 5,000 rounds and the gun is effective out a much greater range than the actual M61.

The Gun HUD Displays

Employing the gun against MiGs requires knowledge of Falcon HUD symbology associated with gun aiming. Aiming the gun at a target moving in three-dimensional space involves some non-trivial physics calculations. The problem of aiming the gun is one of predicting the future event of bullet-target intersection. The F-16 (and the Falcon simulation) solves this problem for the pilot with the *Lead Computing Optical Sight* (LCOS). This aiming device predicts target movement and gives the pilot an aiming reference to shoot the gun at the target. This aiming reference is valid if the shooter (the Falcon) and the target (the MiG) flight parameters remain constant for the time it takes the bullet to get from the shooter to the target. For most gun shoots this is less than one second. The farther you are from the target, the bigger the errors in this system because bullet time of flight, from shooter to target, increases.

Figure 4-2 shows the LCOS display in the Falcon HUD and the SCP. You enter the LCOS mode by pressing the ENTER key on the keyboard until "LCOS" appears on the SCP. The SCP display will change between "AIM9L," "AIM9J," and "LCOS," each time you depress the ENTER key. When you are in LCOS on the SCP, the word "GUN" will also be displayed along with the letters "DGFT" (dogfight) in the lower-right corner of the HUD. These displays inform you that you are in the air-to-air gun mode and the trigger (the SPACEBAR) will shoot the gun, if depressed.

The HUD display in Figure 4-2 shows the Gun Cross, the Aiming Reticle, the Snapshoot Line, and an In Range Cue. The Gun Cross is used in the F-16 to show the pilot the departure line of the bullets. In Falcon, the bullets do not depart the gun barrel at the Gun Cross so this reference is not important in aiming the gun. It does, however, give the pilot a reference in the HUD for the nose position of the aircraft.

The *Aiming Reticle* displayed in the HUD is a set of circles shown in Figure 4-2. The reticle consists of an outside circle and an inside circle with a dot in the middle. This reticle gives the pilot a gun solution based on the constraints listed earlier (shooter and target parameters remain constant for bullet time of flight). The Aiming Reticle gives the pilot a point in the sky where the target should be at the time the bullet reaches it.

The *Snapshoot Line* is the spaghetti-like line depicted in Figure 4-2 that thrashes around the HUD when you maneuver. In the F-16, it is no more than a history of where the Gun Cross has been. In Falcon, it has the

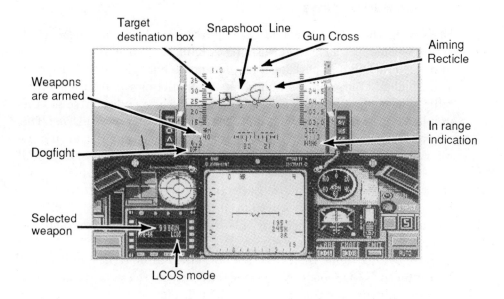

Figure 4-2. LCOS display in the HUD and SCP

similar function of telling the pilot where the bullets would have gone if he had been firing. The Snapshoot Line is not useful in making gun shots because the gun aiming problem is one of predicting a *future event*—where the target is going to be one second from now—rather than one of looking at a *history* of where your bullets would have gone.

Gunning MiGs

An old fighter pilot adage is "MiGs were born to die." The 20-mm gun can certainly help make these words ring true. In order to kill a MiG in the simulation you must get an "IN RNG" cue in the HUD and place the Aiming Reticle over the MiG. After these two conditions are met, you are ready to fire. Chapter 6 will explain the techniques of killing MiGs with the gun.

The Aim-9 Sidewinder Missile

The Sidewinder is a missile that was developed in the 1950s to augment the gun as an air-to-air weapon. During this period in air-to-air weapons development, attempts were being made to shoot down air targets with unguided rockets. The rocket never developed into a dependable weapon but the natural evolution of this technology led to a "guided rocket" or missile. The Sidewinder was the first successful air-to-air missile developed in the world. The first versions of this missile were fielded in the late 1950s and gave the fighter pilot the ability to engage targets outside 2,000 feet, which was the range of the 20-mm gun. It uses infrared energy (heat) from the engine of the target to guide the missile. Because it is an Infrared (IR) guided missile, the launching aircraft is free to maneuver after firing the missile, and does not have to maintain radar lock-on to guide the missile.

The Aim-9L carried by the F-16 is a distant cousin to the early model Sidewinders such as the Aim-9J. It looks almost identical to those early missiles but the similarity ends there. The *L* version of the Sidewinder is a truly revolutionary air-to-air weapon. Many predicted that the first model Sidewinders would change the dynamics of air combat decades ago when they were first introduced. This prophesy went unfulfilled due to poor missile reliability and tight employment parameters of the early model Sidewinder missiles (which included the *J* model). These missiles were of limited use to the fighter pilot in maneuvering combat because they had to be fired within 30 degrees of the target's tail and could be easily out-maneuvered. Conversely, the Aim-9L has made a significant contribution to air combat. This missile can be fired from all aspects and performs very well against maneuvering targets. The Aim-9L has finally given the fighter pilot in a dogfight a dependable way to shoot a target outside of gun range.

Falcon Sidewinder Missiles

The Falcon simulation features two types of Sidewinder missiles. The first of the these is the AIM-9J shown in Figure 4-3. This missile must be fired

Figure 4-3.   AIM-9J

from a stern (or six o'clock position) of the target and has a range of 5 to 11 miles in the Falcon simulation.

The AIM-9L shown in Figure 4-4 has the same range parameters but is not constrained to a stern attack on a target. If you can get the target in your HUD, and an In Range cue (IN RNG), you can shoot the AIM-9L in the Falcon simulation. The *L* missile has a much better probability of killing a maneuvering target than the *J* missile has.

The Sidewinder HUD Displays

Figure 4-5 shows the Sidewinder HUD and SCP displays. Both Sidewinder models (the *J* and *L*) have identical HUD displays in Falcon. The SCP shows which missile you have selected. You can change between missile types with the ENTER key. Remember that pressing the ENTER key moves

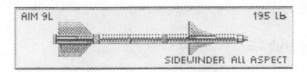

Figure 4-4.   AIM-9L

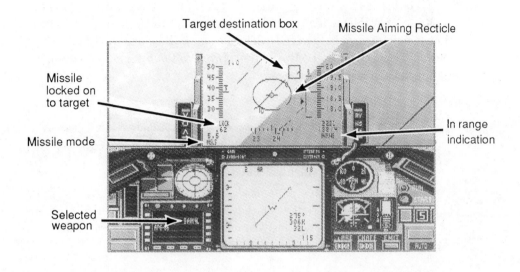

Figure 4-5. Sidewinder HUD displays

the pilot through the air-to-air menu, which includes the Aim-9J, Aim-9L, and the gun LCOS mode. When in the air-to-air missile mode, the letters "MSLS" are displayed in the lower-left corner of the HUD. On the same side of the HUD underneath the airspeed scale is the word "ARM." This changes to the word "LOCK" when your Sidewinders are locked-on to a target. If you have AIM-9 showing in the SCP but do not have either "ARM" or "LOCK" displayed in the HUD, you are out of missiles or are experiencing a malfunction that will prevent you from firing the Sidewinder. Another important missile display in the HUD is the "IN RNG" indicator located in the lower-right corner of the HUD. This display, shown in Figure 4-5, comes into view when the missile can make it to the target.

The most prominent Sidewinder HUD display is a large Aiming Reticle in the center of the HUD. This reticle gives you an aiming reference for shooting the missile. In the Falcon simulation you improve your chances of a missile hit if you fire with the target inside this reticle. Another missile reference is a diamond that appears inside the Target Designator (TD) box. The TD box gives the pilot an aid in the HUD for finding targets. This box appears in the HUD when the radar is locked-on to a target and the target is in the field of view of the HUD. (The TD box will be explained in further detail in the next chapter.) Inside the TD box, a flashing missile diamond will appear when the following conditions are met.

1. The radar is locked-on to a target.

2. The target is in the field of view of the HUD.

3. The AIM-9 missile has locked-on to the target.

There are several other radar-related HUD displays that come into view when you select the Sidewinder. We will cover these displays in the next chapter.

"Fox Two"

When you simulate the shot of a Sidewinder missile on a training sortie you make the radio call, "Fox Two." This lets pilots on both sides of the fight know that a Sidewinder has been fired. This missile is your primary air-to-air weapon in Falcon. The Aim-9L is extremely deadly and affords you great tactical flexibility when fighting MiGs in the simulation. The Aim-9J has more restrictive parameters but at least allows you to engage MiGs several miles out.

FALCON AIR-TO-GROUND SYSTEMS

There are two categories of air-to-ground weapons in Falcon simulation: free-fall (dumb bombs) and guided munitions (missiles). In Falcon you have two types of free-fall munitions: the Mark 84 General Purpose bomb and the Durandel anti-runway bomb. These weapons are referred to as "dumb" and "free-fall" because they are unguided, and the airplane must use on-board aiming systems to drop them with precision. When a bomb is released, it falls to earth on a ballistic trajectory (like a brick) and does not correct itself in flight. A "smart" bomb (such as a laser-guided bomb) makes small corrections in flight as it homes in on reflected laser energy. Missiles such as the Maverick, are self-propelled and guide themselves to the target after lock-on and launch.

Bombs

Bombs are dropped in Falcon using the *Continuously Computing Impact Point* (CCIP) mode. CCIP is a computed delivery mode that takes into account the ballistic characteristics of the bomb and the motion of the aircraft. Using this information, an on- board computer determines the impact point on the ground that the bomb will hit and presents this "bomb solution" to the pilot. The bomb solution is seen in the HUD as an aiming cue or *Pipper,* which is displayed to the pilot as a circle with a dot in it. The pilot then flies the Pipper over the target and drops the bomb. Specific techniques on dropping bombs will be covered in a later chapter. For now it is important that you learn the air-to-ground HUD symbology shown in Figure 4-6.

CCIP Symbology

When you call up either the Mk-84 or the Durandel bombs you will automatically enter the CCIP mode. You call these bombs up in the SCP up by pressing the BACKSPACE key. The BACKSPACE key takes you out of the air-to-air weapons mode and moves the pilot through the air-to-ground weapons rotary, which includes the following selections: the Mk-84 General Purpose bomb, the Durandel anti-runway bomb, the Maverick missile, and the 20-mm gun used for strafing ground targets. Once you have selected the Mk-84 or the Durandel, "CCIP" will appear in the left corner of the HUD. Above "CCIP" you will get the letters "IN RNG" indicating the target is in range. The most important display in the CCIP mode is the Pipper. The Pipper is labeled in Figure 4-6. It is attached to the Bomb Fall Line shown above it. This line connects the Flight Path Marker to the

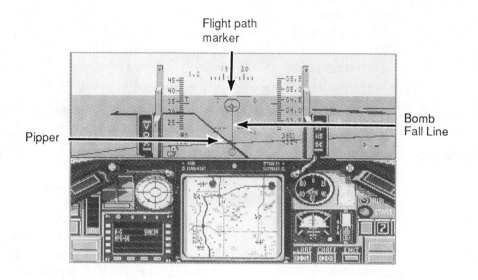

Figure 4-6. CCIP HUD symbology

Pipper and shows the future path over the ground that the Pipper will take as the aircraft moves through the sky. I will explain why this is important when we get to bombing techniques. The Flight Path Marker, the Bomb Fall Line, and the Pipper are the primary displays used by the pilot to drop bombs in Falcon.

There are two additional displays in the CCIP mode that are of some use to the pilot. These are the Delay cue and the Release cue. Figure 4-7 shows these two CCIP pilot cues. The Delay cue is a horizontal line across the vertical Bomb Fall Line. This cue alerts the pilot that the bomb will not release immediately at pickle and the pilot must continue to fly toward the target in order to get bomb release. The other CCIP display is the Release cue. This cue comes into view at pickle, when the Delay cue is present. It tracks down the HUD toward the Flight Path Marker to give the pilot an indication of when the bomb will release. When the Delay cue is present, bomb release occurs when the Release cue reaches the Flight

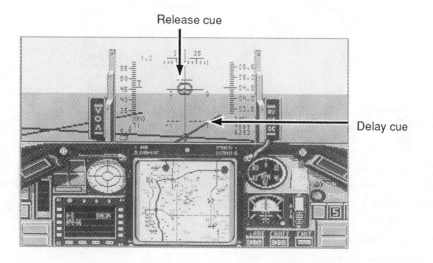

Release cue

Delay cue

Figure 4-7.   CCIP Delay and Release cues

Path Marker. When bombs are released at any time in the CCIP mode the letters "REL" will appear in place of "IN RNG" in the HUD. At pickle (hitting the SPACEBAR), with the Delay cue present, the word "LOCK" will appear and will remain until the bombs are dropped. At that time, "LOCK" will be replaced by the "REL" display.

The Mk-84 General Purpose Bomb

Figure 4-8 shows the Mk-84. This 2000lb bomb can be used in Falcon on all air-to-ground targets. The Mk-84 uses blast and fragmentation to destroy the target. This bomb is particularly deadly against above-ground structures such as buildings and bridges, and is not as effective against runways and tanks. The bomb does not have sufficient penetrating capability to create a deep crater in a runway. Tanks are very difficult to kill

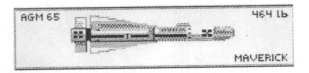

Figure 4-8. Mk-84 General Purpose bomb

with this bomb because you must hit within a few feet of the tank to destroy it. A modern main battle tank is heavily armored and mobile, making it a difficult target for free-fall bombs. While you may not kill a tank with an Mk-84, a 2000lb bomb exploding in close proximity may create a few pacifists inside the tank.

The Durandel Anti-Runway Bomb

The Durandel, shown in Figure 4-9, is brought to you by the same folks that gave you the Maginot Line. This French-built weapon is only slightly better conceived than that infamous World War Two defensive network. The Durandel is designed for cratering runways. Several independent miracles have to take place in order for this to occur.

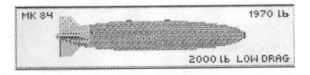

Figure 4-9. Durandel anti-runway bomb

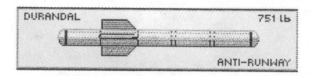

Figure 4-10.   AGM-65 Maverick missile

First, it is dropped like a normal bomb; after release a parachute stabilizes it in a vertical position. Next, a radar fuze senses the ground and at the proper height ignites a rocket motor in the tail end of the bomb, which burrows the bomb into the runway. Finally, the fuze functions, and the bomb explodes creating a deep hole in the concrete. At this point the enemy's runway repair unit, which normally consists of several gumbahs with shovels, quickly converge on the aforementioned hole to fill it in. All in all, it is not a bad weapon for performing the very difficult task of destroying concrete. The Durandel is the best weapon currently available to attack runways, which are very hard to destroy and easy to fix.

The AGM-65 Maverick Missile

The Maverick is depicted in Figure 4-10. This missile is a launch-and-leave weapon that is locked-on to a target visually by the pilot. After lock-on and launch, the missile steers to the target using a guidance system that is on board the missile. Because of this launch-and-leave feature, the pilot does not need to track the target after the missile is fired. The Maverick is a good weapon against tanks and other moving targets due to its ability to self track the target after launch. It can also be used on all other targets in the Falcon "world" (except runways). The Maverick missile has an advertised range of seven to eight miles in the Falcon simulation.

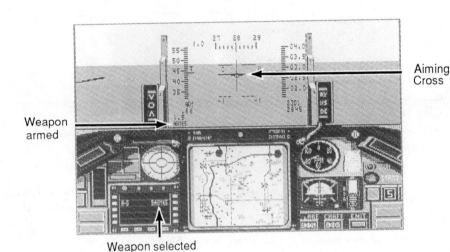

Figure 4-11. Before lock-on Maverick HUD displays

Maverick HUD Symbology

The primary aiming reference used by the pilot for Maverick missile lock-on is the Aiming Cross. Figure 4-11 shows the Aiming Cross and the other "before lock-on" Maverick HUD symbology. You enter the Maverick mode by pressing the BACKSPACE key until "AGM 65" appears in the lower-left corner of the HUD. Above "AGM-65," you will see the word "ARM." Once you line the Aiming Cross up with the target you can command a missile lock-on by hitting the SPACEBAR once. At this time you will get the "after lock-on" HUD symbology shown in Figure 4-12. A "LOCK" indication will replace the word "ARM" in the HUD. In addition, a Target Designator box will appear around the target and a range readout in feet, from your jet to the Target Designator box, will appear in the lower-right corner of the HUD.

Target Designator
box

Missile
locked
on target

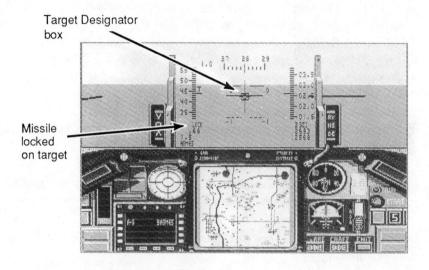

Figure 4-12. After lock-on Maverick HUD displays

The pilot launches the missile after lock-on by hitting the SPACEBAR
a second time. The missile will fire and guide (steer) toward the Target
Designator box. If you hit the SPACEBAR the first time and the missile
locks-on to the wrong target, press the **X** key to reject the lock. This returns
the Maverick to the "before lock-on" mode. You can also use this key to fire
another missile at a different target before the first missile reaches the
target. After firing the first missile, press the **X** key and steer the Aiming
Cross over the next target, lock-on, and shoot.

There are two additional aids to checking your missile lock-on in the
Maverick mode. The first is the radar display. In the Maverick mode the
radar scope will have an Aiming Cross superimposed over the display and
will show ground targets. You can look down at the radar as an alternate
aiming reference.

The second aid is the best way to check your Maverick lock. By pressing the **Q** key, you will transform your entire screen to a view looking out from the Maverick missile itself. You can stay in this mode and "ride" the missile to the target or you can exit this mode by hitting the **3** key. This feature of viewing the target from the perspective of the missile is the best way to get an accurate view of missile lock-on. The F-16 has the same ability to view the target from the missile seeker head, but in the F-16 this picture disappears at missile launch.

The AGM-65 Maverick has a number of control keys that can be used by the pilot. The following is a review of these keys:

BACKSPACE key   Used to enter the air-to-ground weapons mode and move through the different weapons selections.

SPACEBAR   Hitting it once commands missile lock-on. Hitting it again fires the missile.

X key   Used to break missile lock-on and return to "before lock-on" HUD symbology.

Q key   Used to transform the screen to show a view from the missile seeker head.

3 key   Returns the screen to normal from the missile view mode.

20-mm Strafe

Strafing is a good thing to do in an F-16 if you want to experience life as a prisoner of war (POW). The 20-mm gun in the F-16 is an excellent air-to-air weapon, but it lacks the range and killing power to be an effective air-to-ground weapon.

You have to get close to the ground in order to have a chance at hitting and killing a target and, at this low altitude, you are in range of a number of assault rifles carried by a bunch of very mean grunts who have a large stake in the outcome of your attack. The high risk is usually not worth the low payoff associated with 20-mm strafe. There are, however, no absolute

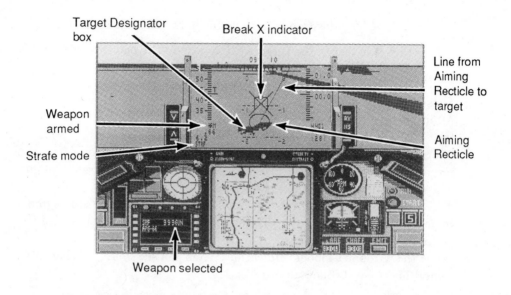

Figure 4-13.   HUD strafe symbology

truths in fighter tactics. If you are down to just your gun, and you need to kill a ground target, then the strafe mode is available to help you out. In the Falcon simulation the gun is an effective weapon for destroying virtually all of the air-to-ground targets. (This is not true in the real F-16.)

Strafe HUD Symbology

Figure 4-13 shows the HUD symbology associated with strafe. The pilot enters this mode by pressing the BACKSPACE key until "STRF" appears in the bottom-left corner of the HUD. The large Aiming Reticle in the middle of the HUD is used to line up on the target. When the target is under the reticle, press the SPACEBAR once to lock-on to the target under the reticle, and press it a second time to fire. You will get the following display when you press the SPACEBAR the first time.

- A Target Designator box will appear around the target.

- A "LOCK" indication will be visible in the left side of the HUD.

- Range in feet to the target will appear in the bottom-right corner of the HUD.

These HUD displays are identical to the "after lock-on" Maverick mode. After lock-on in the strafe mode, a line will connect the Aiming Reticle to the Target Designator box in the HUD. This line gives the pilot an indication of which way to fly the jet to line the Aiming Reticle up with the target. The second time you press the SPACEBAR, the gun fires. The gun will keep firing as long as you hold the SPACEBAR down.

Also shown in Figure 4-13 is the Break X indication. This symbol comes into view to warn you that important parts of your body and the ground are on a collision course. This Break X display is also appropriately called the "Ground Clobber" indication. When you see this X, you better do something about it (like pull up).

CONCLUSION

Falcon can be a complex and frustrating simulation. Don't get mesmerized by all of the different weapons modes and HUD displays. Find a weapon you like to use, and practice until you become dangerous with it (to the enemy, not yourself). The object in Falcon is to quickly get into weapons parameters, destroy the target, and beat it. The next chapter will describe sensors and on-board countermeasures that will help you accomplish this objective.

The Brutal Ambush

5

"...the Fighter with the largest killing zone dictates tactics to the enemy...."

— Col V. Babich
Soviet Fighter Pilot

The modern air combat arena is a very unhealthy place for the blind and ignorant. Throughout the history of air combat, most aircraft have been shot down as a result of a brutal ambush. These targets died relaxed, unaware that they were even under attack. The number of aircraft ambushed, as a percentage of total aircraft destroyed in air-to-air combat, is approximately 90 percent. While high *G* maneuvering combat is still important, historically only a small percentage of the total kills have occurred as a result of the classic dogfight.

The chance of being ambushed today is many times greater than it was in the past, due to greater missile range and improved sensors (primarily radar). The goal in modern air combat is to use your radar to find the enemy and rip his lips off. If you enter today's arena without radar, you're blind. If you have a good radar and you can't use it correctly, you should probably be selling shoes for a living instead of flying fighters. The F-16 has a very effective radar system that can detect targets beyond visual range at all altitudes. The radar scope presents the pilot with a wide range of target information that must be interpreted quickly and correctly in order for the pilot to kill the enemy and survive. The Falcon simulation re-creates some of these complex radar modes.

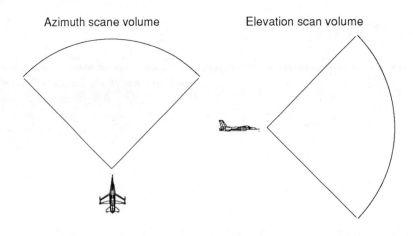

Azimuth scane volume   Elevation scan volume

Figure 5-1.   Radar azimuth and elevation search volumes

FALCON RADAR

Falcon radar information is displayed on the radar scope *and* in the HUD. The radar is always in an auto-lock mode in Falcon and will lock-on to the first target that enters its scan volume. (*Scan volume* is the amount of sky you are searching.) Figure 5-1 depicts the azimuth and elevation scan of the Falcon radar.

There are two primary modes of the radar in the simulation. The first is the search mode. In this mode, shown in Figure 5-2, the radar has not acquired a target, so the target information blocks are filled with *X*s, and no target information is presented. An Artificial Horizon Line is located in

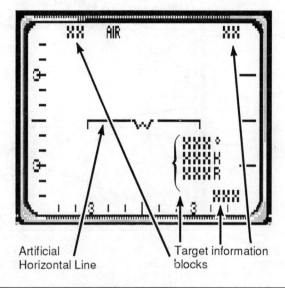

Artificial
Horizontal Line

Target information
blocks

Figure 5-2.   Radar scope in the search mode

the center of the radar and runs horizontally across the scope. This gives the pilot an indication of aircraft roll when he is looking at the radar. The second radar mode is the lock-on mode, which occurs when the radar finds a target and automatically locks-on.

Radar Scope Information

The radar lock-on mode gives the Falcon pilot detailed target information. Figure 5-3 shows the radar scope in the *primary* radar lock-on mode and labels the target information presented in the radar. The target appears in the middle of the scope as a diamond with a single vertical line on each side. The following list explains the information displayed in the radar scope in the lock-on mode shown in Figure 5-3.

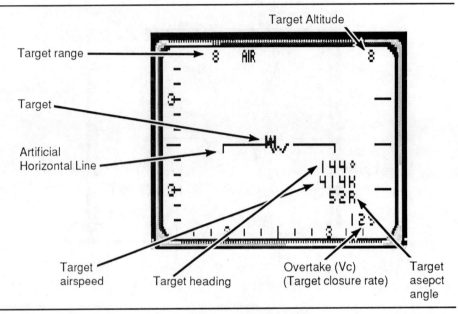

Figure 5-3. Radar scope in the primary lock-on mode

Target Range   Range of the Falcon to the target in miles. Range is presented in the upper-left corner of the radar scope. The target range in Figure 5-3 is eight miles.

Target Altitude   Altitude of the target in thousands of feet. This information is located to the right of the word "air" at the top of the scope. Target altitude in Figure 5-3 is 8,000 feet.

Target Heading   The heading of the target in degrees. Target heading is displayed as the top set of numbers in the target information block in the lower-right part of the scope. There is a degree (°) symbol behind the target heading number. Figure 5-3 shows the target on a heading of 144 degrees.

Target Airspeed   This is the second number down in the target information block, and it tells the pilot how fast the bandit is going. There is a *K,* which stands for Knots, behind the airspeed number. The target airspeed shown in Figure 5-3 is 414 knots.

Target Aspect Angle   Aspect angle is a measure in degrees from the tail of the target to the Falcon. It is the most important information presented by the radar. There is either an *L* or *R* symbol behind the target aspect numbers to denote left or right aspect. Figure 5-3 shows the target as 52 degrees right. Target aspect is very important and difficult to understand at first glance. For this reason we will discuss it in greater detail later in this chapter.

Target Closure Rate (Vc)   This is a measure in knots of how fast you are closing on the target. Target Vc is located in the bottom-right corner of the HUD. In Figure 5-3 it is 129 knots.

All of this information is presented on the radar scope in the primary lock-on mode. The pilot has the option of entering a *secondary* lock-on mode by pressing the F6 key. In this mode the radar range information will be presented in a different format. In the secondary mode, the *range scale* is presented in the top-left corner of the HUD instead of the actual range to the target. In this mode, shown in Figure 5-4, the target moves vertically on the scope to indicate range. The range from the top of the scope to the bottom is whatever number appears in the top-left corner of the radar—ten in Figure 5-4. A target halfway down the scope, for example, with the range scale at ten miles, is five miles from the Falcon. The target in Figure 5-4 is at nine miles. This scale changes automatically in response to changing target range. An additional feature of the secondary lock-on mode is the digital bearing and range to the target that appears in the bottom-left section of the scope. In Figure 5-4, the bearing to the target is 359 degrees and the range is nine miles.

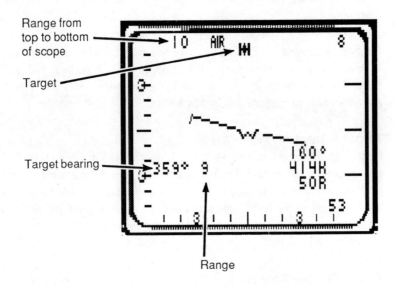

Range from top to bottom of scope

Target

Target bearing

Range

Figure 5-4.   Radar scope in the secondary lock-on mode

HUD Displays

Radar target information is presented in the HUD as well as in the radar scope. Figure 5-5 shows the HUD at radar lock-on and labels the important radar information presented in the HUD.

One of the most useful air-to-air displays in the Falcon simulation is the Target Designator (TD) box located in the HUD. This box appears around the target when the radar is locked-on and the target is in the field of view (FOV) of the HUD. If the radar is locked-on, and the target is *not* in the field of view, a Locator Line will appear at the Gun Cross and point in the direction of the target. Figure 5-6 shows a HUD display with the Locator Line present.

Figure 5-6 also shows another HUD display that presents the pilot with radar data. The Five-Mile-Range Scale, to the right of the Missile Reticle, has a caret that moves vertically to indicate range to the target. Target range presented on the Five-Mile-Range Scale in Figure 5-6 is

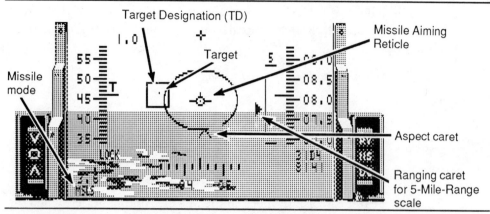

Figure 5-5.   Radar locked on to target in the HUD field of view

approximately four miles. In addition to the Locator Line and Five-Mile-Range Scale, an aspect caret appears on the Missile Aiming Reticle when the radar is locked-on and the pilot is in the Sidewinder missile mode. This aspect caret gives the pilot the same target aspect information that is presented in the radar scope. The caret slides around the Missile Reticle to indicate aspect angle.

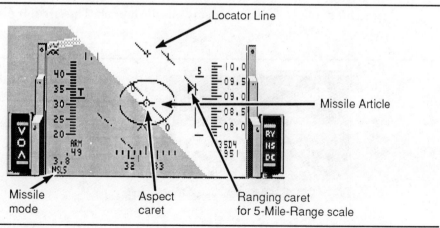

Figure 5-6.   Radar locked on to target in the HUD outside field of view

The following list describes a few different positions of the aspect caret on the Missile Reticle and the target aspect that these positions represent:

Aspect caret clock position	Aspect angle
12 o'clock	180°
3 o'clock	90° left
6 o'clock	0°
9 o'clock	90° right

The aspect caret can be anywhere on the Missile Aiming Reticle when the radar is locked-on to the target. It is important that you can read the aspect at this point in your training even if you don't yet know what to do with it.

THE THREAT INDICATOR

The Threat Indicator is shown in Figure 5-7. This indicator consists of a circular scope and warning lights that illuminate when an enemy missile locks-on ("LCK") and launches ("LNC"). In addition to these lights, the pilot will also get a "beeping" tone to indicate enemy radar lock-on, and a short "scratching" tone to indicate enemy missile launch. The circular display of

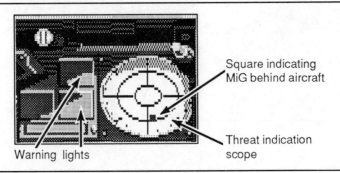

Square indicating
MiG behind aircraft

Threat indication
scope

Warning lights

Figure 5-7. Threat Indicator

the Threat Indicator will show MiGs as small squares at the correct relative azimuth with your jet in the center of the scope. A square at the six o'clock position, as depicted in Figure 5-7, indicates that a MiG is right behind your aircraft. The Threat Indicator will show every MiG that threatens your aircraft, and can also be used to get a bird's-eye view of the air battle. (At the Colonel level only, the scope will not give you range information and will not show MiGs if they have their radars turned off.)

THE INTERCEPT

Interception is the art of starting a fight from beyond visual range and converting your sensor information into dead bandits. The two sensors that we use in Falcon to accomplish this are radar and the Threat Indicator. In the Falcon Air Combat arena the pilot is very limited in what he can see with his eyes. This is the result of the small field of view and the low-res-olution-graphics displays inherent in PC-based simulation. A pilot in an F-16 has a 360-degree view out of the cockpit, and the human eye can see

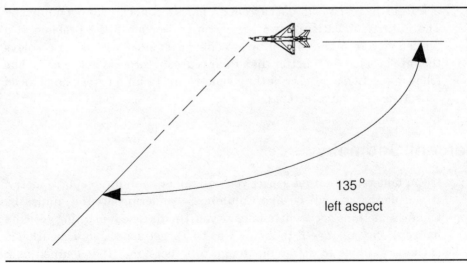

$135°$
left aspect

Figure 5-8.   Target aspect angle

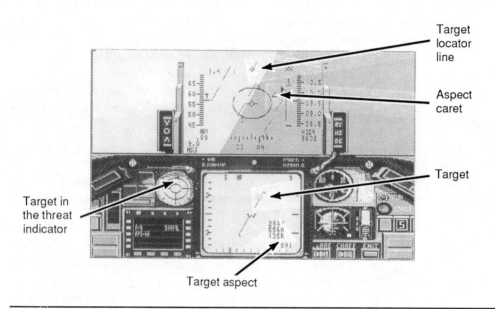

Figure 5-9. Cockpit view of target aspect angle

details in the real world that current graphics technology cannot duplicate. The Falcon simulation, however, partially overcomes the problem of a limited view from the cockpit by providing the "pilot" with other displays that are in some ways better than their real counterparts in the F-16. The following section will describe the geometry and techniques of using Falcon sensors to perform intercepts.

Intercept Geometry

If you understand target aspect you will understand intercept geometry. If you don't, you will be like Columbus, wandering around aimlessly, hoping something good will happen to you. (In his case something good did happen—in your case it probably won't.) Target aspect, as I mentioned earlier, is simple to define but tough to understand. It is defined as a measure in degrees from the tail of the target to your jet. Figure 5-8 shows

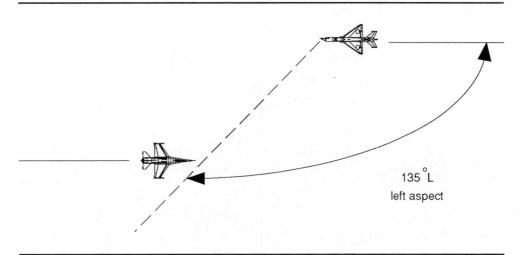

135 °L
left aspect

Figure 5-10.   Target aspect angle

how aspect is measured. In this figure, the target is on the nose of the F-16 at approximately 135 degrees left aspect. Figure 5-9 shows a cockpit view of the same geometry. Note the target aspect in the HUD and in the radar scope. (Be aware that the target aspect displays an *R* where it should display an *L*.) Figure 5-10 shows the exact same aspect angle with the F-16 on a different heading. Your aircraft heading does not have anything to do with *measuring* aspect angle, which is determined by the heading of the *target* only. Aspect angle is important because you instantly know your position in relation to the target when you know aspect angle. If, for example, the HUD indicates 180 degrees of aspect, you would know that you were on the target's nose. Your aircraft may or may not be pointing at the target, but you definitely know that he is pointing at you. In the recent engagement between two Libyan MiGs and two Navy F-14s, the Navy aircrew knew the aspect angle during the intercept and thus knew that the Libyan MiGs continued to come straight at them. Figure 5-11 shows various target aspect angles and the corresponding position of your aircraft.

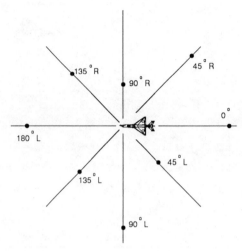

● - Indicates your aircraft position (pointing in any direction)

Figure 5-11. Various target aspect angles and the associated position of the Falcon

Intercept Techniques in Falcon

Now that you have been introduced to target aspect, we will go through some actual intercept techniques. Intercepts are used to arrive in a position of advantage on the target from any distance outside visual range. If you "see" the bandit, you perform Basic Fighter Maneuvers (BFM) and not intercepts (see Chapter 6, "The Spirit of Attack"). Intercepts are flown in phases and the following list explains each step.

Detection Phase   In this phase you are looking for the bad guys. In Falcon you initially detect the bandits by one of three ways:

1. Your Ground Control Intercept (GCI) Controller gives you a range and bearing to the target. This information is shown at the top of the screen. It is usually in the form of descriptive commentary such as "Bluebird (your call sign in Falcon), bogey is at angels 9, bearing 230 degrees, at 19 miles". This GCI call tells the pilot that the bandit (bogey) is at 9,000 feet on a bearing from your aircraft of 230, 19 miles away. Using this information, if you turn the jet to 230 degrees, you should get a radar lock-on.

2. You can pick up the target on your Threat Indicator. This is the worst way to detect a target, but any detection is better than no detection. When you see a target on the scope, turn the jet in the direction of the target and roll out of the turn when the target is on the nose (at the twelve o'clock position on the Threat Indicator scope). The target will now be in the scan volume of the radar and you can get a radar lock.

3. Your radar can detect the target.

The objective of the Detection Phase is to get a radar lock-on. When you accomplish this, move on to the next phase.

Radar Interpretation Phase   In this phase your radar is locked-on to the target, and you must analyze the intercept geometry. To determine the geometry of the intercept, note the target aspect angle and range. If the aspect is *high* (above 120 degrees) you are in the target's *front quarter* (near the target's nose) and are performing a *head-on* intercept. If the aspect is *medium* (60-120 degrees) you are at the target's three or nine o'clock position (depending on left or right aspect). If a medium aspect situation develops, you will roll out behind the bandit if you accelerate to catch him. This occurs because at medium aspect you are in the target's three or nine o'clock position. If you start in this position, the target's forward motion will soon put you behind him. If the aspect is *low* (0-60 degrees), you are in the *stern quarter* (near the target's tail). Since in this case you are already behind the bandit, all you have left to do is accelerate and close the range. The following specific steps should be executed by the pilot based on how far away the target is.

If Target Is Inside Ten Miles   If you are within ten miles of the target at radar lock-on, turn to put the target on the nose. Look at the target's altitude and airspeed while you are in the turn. You should climb or descend to be within 1,000 feet of the target's altitude. In addition, adjust your speed to fly approximately 50 knots faster than the target. If the target is at 350 knots, for example, fly 400 knots. These altitude and airspeed changes are made so that you do not have to make large throttle and stick inputs when you sight the bandit at close range. To put the target on the nose, turn in the direction of the Locator Line in the HUD. Figure 5-12 shows the Locator Line pointing to the right. You would roll the aircraft

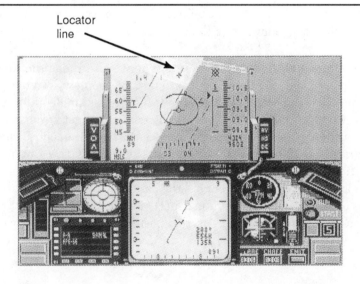

Figure 5-12.   HUD view of target Locator Line

into a right bank and turn to the right until the Locator Line turns into a Target Designator box around the target. At this point just keep the target in the field of view of the HUD until you get into missile range, when you'll see "IN RNG" on the screen.

Target Is Outside Ten Miles   If you are outside the ten miles of the target at radar lock-on, then you must analyze the geometry in order to perform an intercept. Look at target range, airspeed, altitude, and aspect angle. The same airspeed and altitude adjustments that we discussed for targets inside ten miles apply for target ranges outside of ten miles. Descend or climb to 1,000 feet from the target's altitude and change airspeed to fly 50 knots faster than the target. Once you get your altitude and airspeed set, you have to analyze the aspect angle to get a grip on the intercept geometry. There is a number of ways to intercept the MiG in Falcon. This is just one technique based on actual intercept tactics.

If the Aspect Angle Is 120 Degrees or Less   Turn to put the target on your nose and accelerate to get 100 knots of Vc on the target. Remember this number is read at the bottom-right corner of the radar scope (see Figure 5-3). You have already adjusted your airspeed to fly 50 knots faster than the target so this won't require a big throttle change.

If the Aspect Angle Is Greater Than 120 Degrees   Note your heading and turn 30 degrees opposite the target aspect to get *lateral displacement,* or turning room, on the target. For example, if the aspect is 150 degrees right, turn 30 degrees left. This turning room is the distance from the target needed to convert to the target's six o'clock. Figure 5-13 shows a bird's-eye view of the intercept and why you turn opposite the target aspect. In Figure 5-13, if the F-16 turned in the same direction as the aspect angle, he would decrease his lateral displacement and would pass the bandit head-on instead of rolling out at the target's six o'clock.

After completing this maneuver, the range will decrease. When you're eight miles from the target, turn to put the target on your nose. If the aspect angle is medium to low, you are converting to the bandit's stern quarter. The enemy MiGs in Falcon have a nasty habit of running an intercept on you at the same time you're intercepting them. If this happens, the aspect

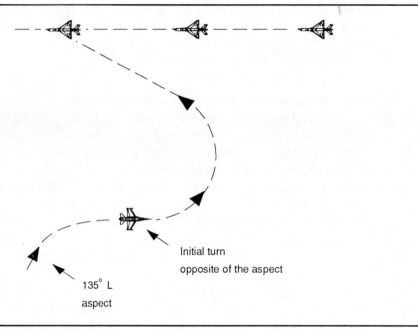

Initial turn

opposite of the aspect

135° L

aspect

Figure 5-13.   Bird's-eye view of the intercept

will stay high and you will pass them head-on (at high aspect). The next chapter will discuss maneuvering after a head-on pass.

If the target is not maneuvering against you, the turn you made opposite the target aspect will give you lateral displacement and allow you to convert to the MiG's six o'clock.

The Kill Phase   At some point during the intercept, you will get an in range ("IN RNG") indication for your Sidewinder missile. As soon as you get this indication, shoot. The whole idea behind the intercept is to place your jet in a position to kill the bandit. Figure 5-14 shows an outside view of the Falcon firing a Sidewinder.

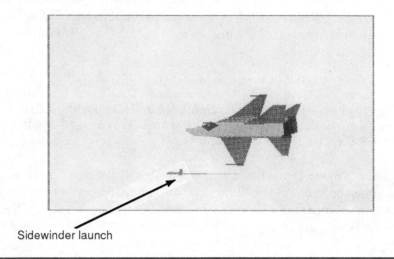

Sidewinder launch

Figure 5-14.   Falcon Sidewinder launch

FALCON ELECTRONIC COUNTERMEASURES

Electronic Countermeasures (ECM) are techniques that are used to deny the enemy the use of his radar and infrared systems. In Falcon these systems are used by the enemy for detection and missile guidance. Falcon ECM systems include the Threat Indicator, the chaff and flare dispenser, and the externally mounted ALQ-131 jamming pod.

The Threat Indicator

We have already covered some of the capabilities of the Threat Indicator. The following list describes some Threat Indicator signals and what they mean to the pilot.

- The Missile Lock Light is seen on the Threat Indicator Warning Panel as a flashing "LCK". This indication tells the pilot that a radar-guided missile has locked-on to you. The lock ("LCK") indication always precedes a missile launch ("LNC") indication for radar-guided missiles.

- When an enemy missile is launched with your name on it, you will receive a flashing "LNC" indication on the Threat Indicator Warning Panel. If you get a *missile launch* indication without first getting a *missile lock* indication, then you are being engaged by a IR-guided SAM.

The Threat Indicator is the single most important piece of ECM equipment on your Falcon. Without it, you cannot detect an enemy missile attack. Remember the words of that gnarled-up, old back- seater: "Nothing good will ever happen to you without detection".

The Chaff and Flare Dispenser

The Falcon is equipped with a dispenser that ejects either chaff or flares. A chaff bundle consists of small strips of metal that reflect radar energy. These chaff bundles rapidly blossom when ejected from the airplane and are effective in decoying radar-guided missiles. Flares are a pyrotechnic device that burn to create infrared energy when dispensed to decoy IR-guided SAMs. Figure 5-14 shows the chaff and flare indicators on the front cockpit.

The appropriate indicators illuminate anytime you dispense chaff or flares, and the counters under the chaff and flare lights count down to show you the amount remaining. You dispense chaff by hitting the DEL key. You get one bundle of chaff each time you press the DEL key, and the counter will decrement by one. The flare dispenser is identical in operation to the chaff dispenser except that you press the INS key to eject a flare. The Falcon has 30 chaff bundles and 30 flare cartridges, which should be used *anytime* you are under attack. You do not get any extra style points for dying with chaff and flares on board your jet, so use them when you need them.

Figure 5-15.   Chaff, flare, and jamming pod indicator

The ALQ-131 Jamming Pod

The ALQ-131 jamming pod is an external ECM pod used to decoy radar-guided missiles. In the Falcon simulation you should try to fly with the pod anytime you expect to tangle with enemy SAMs. To turn the pod on, press the **E** key. The **E** key toggles the pod on and off, and when you hit this key, the "ECM" light located under the word "EMIT" will illuminate. Figure 5-15 depicts this light, which is located to the right of the chaff and flare indicators. When you press the **E** key with the "ECM" light on, you will extinguish the light and turn the pod off. The pod is an effective system for countering enemy radar missiles but it does highlight your position so turn it on only when you get a "LCK" indication, and turn it off as soon as the "LCK" indication disappears.

We will discuss the tactical use of all ECM systems in the next few chapters.

SITUATION AWARENESS

Situation Awareness (SA) is the pilot's ability to predict the future course of the air battle based on the information at hand. Situation awareness is gained by listening to the radio, interpreting sensors such as radar, and looking out of the cockpit. A pilot with good SA is like King Kong, and has the ability to dominate the air battle. A pilot with poor SA is like Little Bo Peep, and has very little ability to influence the fight. The Falcon pilot must learn to acquire good Situation Awareness. The next chapters will cover specific Falcon fighting techniques that will help transform you from the hunted to the hunter.

THE SPIRIT OF ATTACK

6

"Only the spirit of attack, born in a brave heart, will bring success to a fighter aircraft, no matter how highly developed it may be."

—Adolf Galland

The F-16 Fighter Weapons School was a grueling four-month program of intensive flight and academic training on weapons and tactics for F-16 instructor pilots. Intimidation and general abuse were the standard methods of replicating the stress of combat. The Weapons School sought to produce graduates with a thorough knowledge of advanced fighter concepts, gained in high intensity "combat" sorties. Life at the School definitely made you wish for the alternative of real combat.

On this day, we huddled like sheep in the corner of a trailer that was the temporary home of the newly established F-16 Weapons School. We were getting a Basic Fighter Maneuvers (BFM) phase briefing from a particularly nasty individual who went by the call sign of "Doofal." He mentioned that if we were going to wash out of the course, it would probably be in the BFM phase. He told us also that in the likely event that we did wash out we would be deemed too dangerous to fly, even as a passenger on an airliner, so the Air Force would issue us a bus ticket back to our home base. I wasn't sure if he was kidding or not, but I didn't relish the idea of riding the "Hound" from Nellis AFB in Las Vegas to MacDill AFB in Tampa. I paid attention to the briefing.

For my first BFM ride, I drew one of the toughest air-to-air instructors at the Weapons School. Skip was a fairly even-tempered guy on the ground but a *mean* son of a gun in the air. (Later in the course I would fly with Skip on the Maverick ride described in Chapter 4.)

A few months prior to our arrival an Israeli F-16 ace had visited the Weapons School and fought Skip one-on-one. Skip had gun- tracked him in all three engagements from offensive, defensive, and head-on starting positions. This fact, plus a vision of a bus ticket to Tampa with my name on it, stayed on my mind as we started our first engagement.

The first two BFM rides at the Weapons School placed the student on offense. The mission objective of these rides was to stay behind the instructor and fire a valid missile or gun shot. I managed to do this on the first two engagements but on the third engagement I got spit out. The fight developed quickly into a nose high flat scissors with both aircraft climbing straight up. (A scissors is a maneuver where two aircraft are aligned abreast and are turning back and forth into each other, or scissoring, in order to get the advantage. The pilot who maneuvers the nose of his aircraft up first will slow his forward ground track and get a six o'clock on his opponent.) As the airspeed plummeted, the controls became less and less effective until Skip and I were staring at each other across a few hundred feet of thin air, and just "riding the Pratt and Whitney blowtorch." When the airspeed fell to double digits the nose of my jet started falling back through the horizon. Skip had somehow managed to hold his nose up a split second longer than I did, and he ended up behind me at close range. The airspeed started to climb when the fight went downhill, and I guns jinked as Skip moved into firing position. My jink-out delayed the kill shoot but the fight ended soon after when Skip called a tracking gunshot.

In the mission debrief back at the base all three engagements were dissected in excruciating detail as Skip pointed out where I had blundered. I figured I'd done alright by staying behind him in two of the three engagements since even the Israeli ace hadn't done as well, but I was wrong. At the end of the debriefing Skip said, "Well, it was a weak ride but I'll pass you anyway. You'll have to do better on the next ride." "Have to do better?" I thought. I had flown the best BFM ride of my life, and I wasn't sure how I was going to improve. As it turned out, I did pass the next ride and somehow made it through the entire course, even though the specter of the bus ticket arose again on a few occasions.

Part of what I learned about F-16 BFM during that course will be covered in this chapter. BFM is the foundation of all air-to-air and air-to-ground missions. You employ BFM every time you mix it up with MiGs or roll in to attack ground targets so you must understand BFM in the Falcon simulation to understand what is going on.

BFM is divided into three distinct learning blocks: offensive, defensive, and head-on maneuvering. This chapter will focus on the mechanics of maneuvering when you are within visual range of the MiG. To stay behind the bandit in Falcon requires the same skills and knowledge required in the real jet. There is no easy, straightforward BFM technique that applies only to the Falcon game. Since the simulation is governed by the aerodynamic principles that govern actual air combat, the successful simulator pilot must learn the same BFM principles that the fighter pilot does.

ENERGY FOR AIRCRAFT POSITION

Basic Fighter Maneuvers are nothing more than the exchange of energy for aircraft position. Energy, for the purpose of our discussion, is fighter speed and altitude. The goal of *offensive maneuvering* in the simulation (and in the real F-16) is to remain behind an adversary and get in a position to shoot your weapons. In *defensive maneuvering* you must turn your jet so that the bandit is no longer in a position to shoot his weapons at you. In *head-on maneuvering* you must get behind the bandit, starting from a neutral position.

When you execute maneuvers to accomplish these objectives you will invariably bleed off or expend energy. Pulling *G*s and turning causes all aircraft to slow down or lose altitude, or both. In this discussion we will describe the geometry of the fight and the specific maneuvers needed to be a successful air-to-air Falcon pilot.

BFM Is Flown in the Future

Many discussions of BFM emphasize maneuvers as if they were cards or chess pieces played in a game of moves and countermoves. Modern aerial warfare, however, is actually closer to a wrestling match. It is a fluid contest hinging on the quickness of the opponents' reactions. The Falcon simulation has taught you by now that you are in a dynamic fight with little time for creative thought or slow analysis. Aerial combat requires reaction. As a rule, fighter pilots are not too bright on the ground; in the air, however, we are brilliant for very short periods of time. This period of time is the split second it takes to analyze the situation and react. Because changes occur so rapidly during BFM, you must constantly follow these four basic steps:

1. *Observe* the bandit.

2. *Predict* a future position in space for the bandit, based on your observation.

3. *Maneuver* your jet in response to this prediction.

4. *React* to changes in the situation as you execute your maneuvers.

You can tell from this list that BFM is flown in the future and not in the present. You must constantly predict the bandit's *future position,* or where the MiG will be a few seconds from the time you observe it, and fly your jet based on this prediction.

BFM GEOMETRY

In order to perform BFM the pilot must understand the spatial relationship to the target from four perspectives: positional geometry, attack geometry, the weapon envelope, and the control zone.

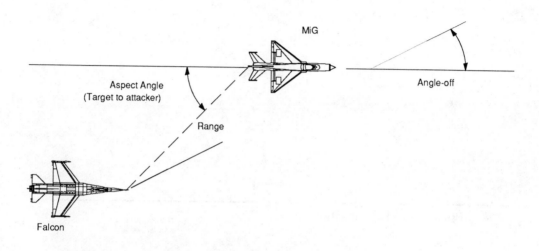

Figure 6-1. Angular relationship between two aircraft

Positional Geometry

Range, aspect angle, and angle-off are the terms used to describe one aircraft's position relative to another. These terms, depicted in Figure 6-1, define the angular relationship between two aircraft. This angular relationship in turn tells you how much of a position advantage or disadvantage you have.

Range is the distance between your jet and the bandit.

Aspect angle is the number of degrees measured from the tail of the target to your aircraft. Aspect angle is important because it tells you how far away you are in degrees from the stern of the target (the desired position).

Angle-off is the difference, measured in degrees, between your heading and the bandit's heading. This angle tells you relative fuselage align-

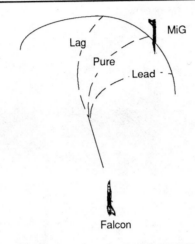

Figure 6-2.   Pursuit options

ment. For example, if the angle-off were 0 degrees you would be on a parallel heading with the bandit and your two fuselages would be aligned. If the angle-off were 90 degrees, your fuselage would be perpendicular to that of the bandit.

Attack Geometry

Attack geometry describes the path that the offensive fighter takes as he converges on the bandit. When you start an attack there are three distinct paths or pursuit courses that you can follow. These are pure pursuit, lag pursuit, or lead pursuit. If you are pointing directly at the bandit you are flying a *pure pursuit* course. If you are pointing behind the bandit you are in *lag pursuit,* and if your nose is out in front of the bandit you are in *lead pursuit.* Figure 6-2 shows these different pursuit options available when attacking the bandit. You can tell in the Falcon simulation what pursuit course you are flying by the position of the Flight Path Marker in relation

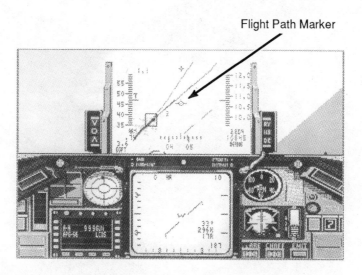

Flight Path Marker

Figure 6-3. Cockpit view of lead pursuit

to the MiG. Figure 6-3 shows a lead pursuit course. Notice the Flight Path Marker out in front of the bandit. If you were in pure pursuit, the Flight Path Marker would be right over the bandit. If you were in lag pursuit the Flight Path Marker would be behind the bandit.

The Weapons Envelope

The weapons envelope is the area surrounding the bandit in which you are in parameters to shoot a missile or the gun. The parameters are defined by range, aspect angle, and angle-off. The dimensions and position of this area are dictated by the type of weapons that you are carrying. If your jet is loaded with all-aspect Aim-9Ls, the envelope looks like a doughnut, with

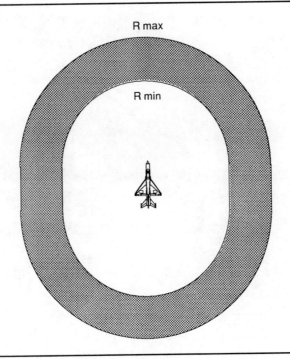

Figure 6-4. Aim-9L weapons envelope

the inside circle being minimum range (Rmin) and the outside circle being maximum range (Rmax). Figure 6-4 shows a shaded doughnut area that represents the Aim-9L weapons envelope. If you are carrying an Aim-9J stern-aspect missile, the vulnerable area is cone-shaped as shown in Figure 6-5. These two missile envelopes are so different because the seeker heads of the missiles work differently. The older *J* model Sidewinder seeker head can only pick up IR energy from the target's engine from the stern or rear of the target. The *L* model's seeker head can sense IR energy from the target's engine from all aspects (360 degrees).

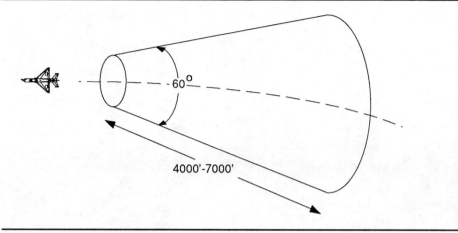

Figure 6-5. Aim-9J weapons envelope

The Control Zone

The control zone, also called *the elbow,* is the area behind the bandit where you can establish a stable position in which to employ your weapons. From this position it is relatively easy to remain behind the bandit and in control. (This spot is called the elbow because when fighter pilots describe air combat with their hands, the elbow of the arm that is showing the bandit's motion is the approximate position of the control zone.)

In the Falcon simulation, this position is about 3,000-4,000 feet behind the maneuvering MiG when the MiG is at corner velocity. *Corner velocity* is the speed at which an aircraft can turn the fastest, tightest turn—for the MiG in Falcon approximately 400 knots. As the bandit bleeds off energy and slows down, the control position moves closer to the MiG. A MiG at 200 knots, for example, has a control position of 1,500-2,000 feet. This is because the MiG cannot generate a very high turn rate at this slow speed, so you can fly much closer to the bandit and still stay in control.

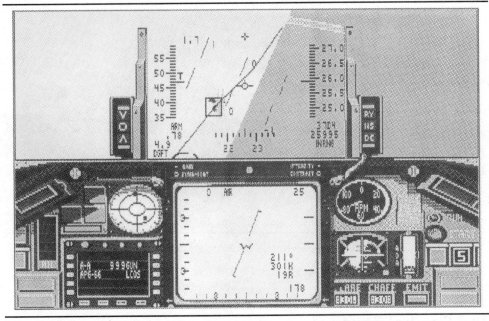

Figure 6-6.   The control position (the elbow)

BFM is flown to arrive at the elbow of the bandit with 100 knots of overtaking airspeed (overtake), and within 30 degrees of the bandit's heading (angle-off). Figure 6-6 shows the view from the cockpit when the Falcon is in the control position on the MiG. Note that this position also places you in the weapons envelope for your Aim-9J.

BFM MECHANICS

You will recall that aircraft maneuvers consist of roll, turn, and acceleration. Roll is used to position your lift vector. The nose of the aircraft will turn in the direction of the lift vector once you put some *G*s on the jet.

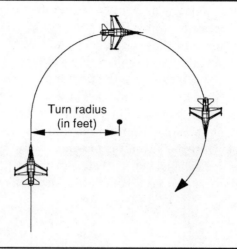

Figure 6-7.   Aircraft turn circle

Offensive BFM involves turning your jet to solve aspect, angle-off, and overtake problems created by the bandit's turns. Unfortunately, this is no easy task. You must know precisely where and how to turn in order to successfully solve these problems and remain behind the bandit. To learn this, we will discuss the characteristics of a turning jet.

Turn Rate and Radius

Two characteristics of a turning aircraft that a fighter pilot must understand are turn radius and turn rate. *Turn radius* is simply a measure of how tightly your jet is turning. If you were looking down on the aircraft as it turned, turn radius would be the distance from the center of your *turn circle* to the aircraft, measured in feet. Figure 6-7 shows this circle.

The equation for turn radius is

$$TR \text{ (turn radius)} = V^2/gG$$

V is the aircraft's velocity in feet per second. Little g is gravity and big G is the Gs the aircraft is pulling.

It is not important that you understand how to compute turn radius, but it is important that you realize that velocity is squared in the turn radius equation. This means that the fighter pilot must control his velocity (airspeed) to control his turn radius. The equation also includes aircraft Gs. The more Gs that you pull, the tighter the turn.

Turn rate is the second important characteristic of turning the jet. Turn rate is how fast the aircraft is moving around the turn circle we just talked about, or how fast an aircraft can move its nose. Turn rate is measured in degrees per second and is also dependent on Gs and airspeed.

Turn rate = K G/V

K is a constant and big G and V are again, respectively, Gs and velocity. This equation tells the fighter pilot that the highest Gs possible, at the lowest airspeed, gives the best turn rate. Turn rate is very important in BFM because it is a measure of how fast you can put your nose on the bandit. Since you have to put your nose on the MiG to shoot at it, you obviously require a fast turn rate.

You will never master Falcon BFM unless you can control your airspeed. A good overall combat airspeed in the Falcon simulation is 400-450 knots. If you fly faster than this when you are trying to turn, the result will be a very large turn radius and a slow turn rate. Flying faster than 450 is not a good idea in a turning fight. If you fly slower than 400 knots, your turn radius will be small but your rate will go down because you will be unable to achieve high Gs at a slow speed. Remember, the higher the Gs, the faster the turn.

To achieve the proper airspeed at the Lieutenant or Captain level in an air-to-air configuration, set the RPM at about 80 percent. Above the Captain level the engine characteristics change, and you must set the power in the 90 percent-Mil range to maintain this airspeed. Remember that this is the airspeed you are striving for once you start a sustained turning engagement with MiGs. In an air-to-ground configuration (with bombs or Mavericks loaded), or in the presence of SAMs, you will want to keep your speed up to at least 550 knots. If you start turning with a MiG loaded with bombs, you will soon bleed down your airspeed to the desired fighting speed of 400-450 knots.

Acceleration

Acceleration is how fast you go faster. This is very important because BFM usually results in energy bleed off, and a fighter must be able to regain this energy by acceleration. The best way to accelerate in the Falcon simulation is to light the afterburner (AB), roll the wings level with the horizon, and head for the ground in about 20 degrees of dive. If you are playing at the Lieutenant level you don't have to dive because gravity is not a factor.

FALCON OFFENSIVE BFM

Now that we have covered the geometry of the fight and some basic mechanics we will discuss specific offensive, defensive, and head-on Falcon maneuvers. In an air-to-air fight you are forced to execute specific maneuvers in response to the bandit's. In offensive maneuvering, BFM must be performed whenever the bandit turns into you and creates aspect, angle-off, and range problems.

The BFM that you can actually execute in Falcon is constrained due to the limits on what you can "see" in the simulation. All simulations have restrictions and Falcon is no exception. The MiGs in the simulation are difficult to see until they are at very close range. Outside of 3,000 feet, it is very difficult to tell what the MiG is doing and to judge the geometry of the fight. Because of this, most fights with the MiG result in a confusing "fur ball" of high-speed passes and missile engagements at ranges greater than one mile. You know you did good when the MiG blows up, but you're not sure what happened or why. In this section we will discuss methods for going through the basic BFM steps of observing, predicting, maneuvering, and reacting. We will also highlight some simulation "work arounds" that will help you execute the offensive BFM needed to win.

Setting Up the Fight

For this training mission set up the Lieutenant level, Black Bandit mission, and set the number of MiGs to one. After takeoff, pull the power back to 80 percent to establish your airspeed at 400-450 knots. Climb to 25,000 to 35,000 feet and select the Autopilot mode by hitting the **A** key. The word "auto" will appear in the cockpit when this mode is selected. The Autopilot mode will put the computer in control of your jet. In autopilot, the Falcon will automatically fly the mission that you have selected. When MiGs appear, the autopilot will fight the MiGs and strive to fly your Falcon to the six o'clock position on the MiG.

Flying to the Elbow

Use the autopilot to get behind a MiG. Once you are established at the MiG's six o'clock, select the Sidewinder missile mode and note the position of the aspect caret in the HUD. Figure 6-8 shows the Falcon established behind the MiG. As the autopilot flies the jet, adjust the throttle to match the MiG's speed as closely as you can. Note that the MiG is turning, and that the Falcon turns in response to this movement. That is essentially the solution to the BFM problem of a turning MiG in the Falcon simulation. When the MiG turns, you turn. Turn the autopilot off by pressing the **A** key again. You should now be in position to practice flying the jet yourself. The following steps will cover when and how you turn the Falcon to stay behind the MiG:

1. Use the HUD, the radar scope and the Threat Indicator to *observe* the MiG. If you cannot determine the MiG's direction of turn by looking out of the HUD and seeing him, look at your Threat Indicator and you will see the MiG moving around the circle, either clockwise or counterclockwise.

2. When you observe the direction of turn for the MiG, *predict* his movement across the sky and start a turn in the same direction. For example, if the MiG moves to the left in your HUD or on your Threat Indicator, you turn left.

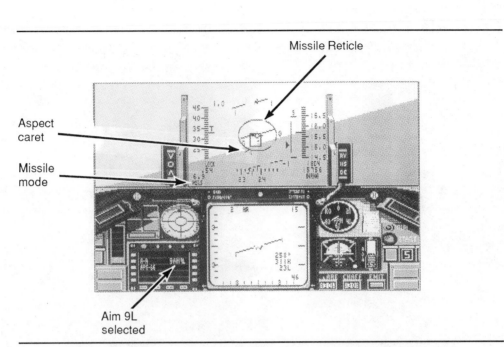

Missile Reticle

Aspect caret

Missile mode

Aim 9L selected

Figure 6-8.   Sidewinder HUD symbology

3. As the MiG starts turning out in front of you, *maneuver* to place the Flight Path Marker out in front of the MiG (lead pursuit) and start pulling five to seven Gs. Adjust the airspeed to gain 50 knots of closure (read closure in the bottom-right corner of your radar scope). Figure 6-9 shows this position on the MiG.

4. You must now observe the movement of the MiG in your HUD to determine how you will *react*. The MiG will do one of three things in relation to your Flight Path Marker:

   • If the MiG stays in the same spot in the HUD, you are matching the MiG's turn rate and will close the range and fly to the elbow. Just keep doing what you're doing and prepare to strike a blow for freedom. If you are armed with Sidewinder missiles, shoot. If you are "winchester" (have run out of Sidewinders), switch to guns and fire when you can see the delta

MiG   Flight Path Marker

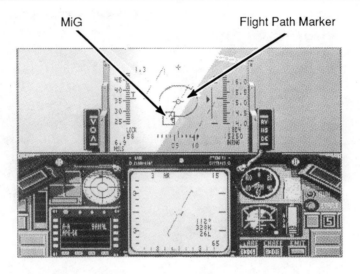

Figure 6-9.   HUD view at the start of the attack

wings of the MiG. Figure 6-10 shows this gun-firing position on the MiG.

- If you pull the Flight Path Marker to lead and the MiG moves rapidly across your HUD and back under your nose, ease off the *G*s and let him fly back into view. In this case you are pulling too much lead for the MiG's present turn rate. Once you regain a tally ho, put the Flight Path Marker behind the bandit in lag pursuit. Figure 6-11 shows a lag pursuit position on the MiG. In this figure, you are pointing behind the MiG, and when the range closes, the MiG will start moving away from you in the direction of the turn. When this occurs pull your nose back to lead pursuit and again get ready for a gunshot. In both of these cases you may pass through Sidewinder parameters and be able to fire.

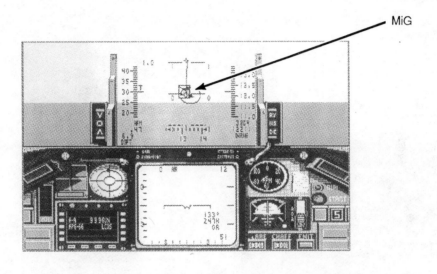

Figure 6-10.   Cockpit view of gun-tracking position

- If the MiG moves through the Flight Path Marker and you go from lead to lag pursuit, you are not matching the MiG's turn rate and will overshoot. An *overshoot* is when you fly past the MiG and are in danger of going out in front of him. Figure 6-12 shows a bird's-eye view of an overshoot situation. The solution to this problem is to turn the Falcon as hard as possible and check your airspeed. If you are over 450 knots, you will overshoot the MiG every time. (Remember velocity is squared in the rate and radius equations.) If you do overshoot in Falcon, don't worry; just keep turning in the direction of the MiG and you will get behind him.

All of these steps are designed to get you to the elbow of the MiG. You must be aware of your airspeed and closure at all times when flying these maneuvers. The next section will cover what to do once you've cleverly trapped a MiG at *your* six o'clock.

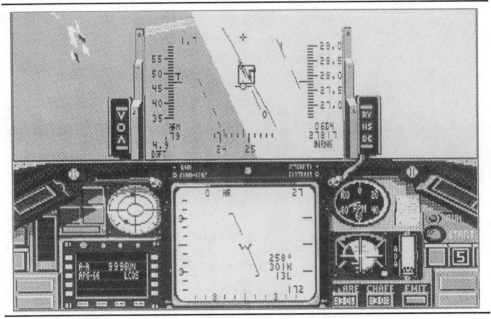

Figure 6-11. Cockpit viw of lag pursuit

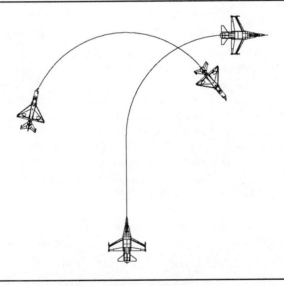

Figure 6-12. Bird's-eye view of an overshoot

FALCON DEFENSIVE BFM

You are not sure what went wrong but there he is, a bloodthirsty National Socialist, at your six o'clock. Before you reach for the ejection handle, let's discuss your options in the Falcon simulation. Defensive BFM is a very easy concept to grasp in Falcon (and in the F-16). A will to survive is a pilot's most essential characteristic. The geometry of the defensive fight is very simple and the maneuvers are equally straightforward. You must be able to execute them, however, while you are under both mental pressure and the physical duress of violent high-G maneuvering. Defensive maneuvering requires patience, stamina, and optimism. Keep asking yourself, "Self, am I still alive?" If the answer is yes, keep fighting.

Maneuver and ECM

The first thing you need to do on defense is create BFM problems for the bandit. From our previous discussion, you know how difficult it is to stay behind a hard-turning bandit. In order to give the enemy the same trouble you experienced, execute the following procedures for the following defensive situations:

Missile Launch   Pay close attention to the Threat Indictor. If you see or hear a missile launch indication at any time during the simulation stop what you are doing, and execute the following procedures:

1. Dispense chaff and flares and turn your jamming pod (the ALQ-131) on if you have one.

    * Chaff: press the DEL key

    * Flares: press the INS key

    * Jamming Pod: Press the **E** key

    Don't try to interpret which type of missile the enemy is firing; you will have plenty of time to ponder that in the POW camp if your defensive reactions don't work.

2. While you are using your ECM, you must also put maximum *G*s on the jet as rapidly as possible to give the enemy missile a difficult target. Again, don't sweat which way to turn, just do it. A missile launch in the Falcon simulation requires you to move quickly.

If you get a lock-on indication before you get a launch, dispense chaff only and turn the pod on. In this case you have more time to maneuver the jet against the MiG.

MiG at Six O'clock   In the case where the MiG is at your six o'clock and you get a lock-on indication or no indication, look at the Threat Indicator to figure out the direction of your defensive turn and execute the following steps:

1. If the bandit is on the right side of scope, turn right. If he is on the left, turn left. In the rare instance that you can actually see the bandit, turn towards the bandit.

2. Roll to set your wings at approximately 80-90 degrees of bank and start a hard turn into the bandit at *maximum G*. Turn with as much *G* as the jet will give you.

3. Next, look at the Threat Indicator, note the direction of movement of the bandit on the scope, and react accordingly:

   • If the bandit is moving toward your twelve o'clock position, your turn is working. You are giving the bandit a problem he can't solve, and he is moving out in front of you. Keep turning until he gets to your nose and your radar locks-on. At this point you are no longer on the defensive but are now probably flying offensive or head-on BFM. Figure 6-13 shows a bird's-eye view of a successful defensive turn.

   • If you turn hard into the bandit and he does not move to the twelve o'clock position on the Threat Indicator, you are in for a real tussle. The first thing to do is to check your airspeed. This is always a good thing to do in any air-to-air situation when things aren't going well. If you are flying faster than 450 knots, slow down to give your jet a tighter turn circle. If you

Figure 6-13.   Defensive turn

are flying slower than 350 knots and you are not in AB, get there by pressing the / key and then the < key to get all 5 stages of the AB. This should get your airspeed up to 450; if it doesn't and you still have external stores on the jet, jettison them by pressing CTRL-K. This will clean off the entire aircraft by dropping everything that you have hanging on the jet *if* you are in a game level above Major.

Hopefully, one of these steps solved your problem and the bandit is now moving forward toward the twelve o'clock position on the Threat Indicator. If not, there is nothing more that you can do but keep turning and hope he runs out of gas or makes a mistake. I wish I could give you a "magic move" that would put the bandit out in front of you but unfortunately none exists. The important thing to remember is that a MiG at six o'clock is better than no MiG at all to a confident and aggressive fighter pilot.

FALCON HEAD-ON BFM

This BFM is flown after passing the bandit head-on. You have the option at this point to separate from from the MiG. You also have the option to turn and duke it out with him. If your mission is to kill the bandit, you have to know how to fight head-on BFM. Falcon head-on BFM is very easy to execute but difficult to understand. The following steps will help you take a head-on situation and convert it into an offensive one:

1. Use the Threat Indicator, the HUD, and the radar scope to point at the bandit (or place him at your twelve o'clock position).

2. When you get an in range (IN RNG) indication in the HUD, shoot a Sidewinder. If the Sidewinder doesn't work, switch to guns and shoot when you get inside two miles.

3. Stay heads up for a missile launch indication on your Threat Indicator as the MiG approaches. Execute the steps we discussed in the defensive BFM section if you do get a launch indication. There should be no doubt in your mind; when somebody shoots at you, you're defensive.

4. When you "see" the MiG fly past you, or when you see the MiG on the Threat Indicator move toward your six o'clock, start a hard turn at five to seven Gs in the direction of the MiG. Figure 6-14 shows a bird's-eye view of a head-on pass with the MiG. In the Falcon simulation it is not important which way you turn at the pass; it is only important that you initiate the turn quickly after passing the MiG.

5. After starting a hard turn into the MiG, keep the turn coming until you get the MiG in your HUD again. Analyze the aspect and

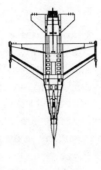

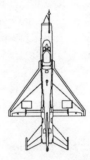

Figure 6-14.   Head-on pass

if it is high (above 120 degrees), you are still in a head-on fight. Go back to step one. If the aspect angle is medium or low, you are winning the manly contest of head-on BFM. Just keep pulling hard in the MiG's direction and you will soon be behind it.

6. Anytime you get very confused, remember this: always turn in the direction of the MiG. If you can't think of anything else to do, just keep turning into him, using the Threat Indicator as a reference.

We have discussed maneuvering from offensive, defensive, and head-on situations. The goal of all this is to survive the attack of the bandit and shoot him down. To do this you need weapons. The next section will cover Falcon air-to-air weapons employment.

Sidewinders

The Sidewinder in Falcon is an easy weapon to use. We will discuss both the *J* and the *L* missiles together even though they perform differently. We have already addressed Sidewinder symbology in the HUD and shown charts for the Sidewinder missile envelopes earlier in this chapter. What we will cover in this section is the tactical use of the missile in the Falcon simulation. You should always fly with the Aim-9L Sidewinder missile selected if you have one loaded. If you don't have an *L* model Sidewinder, fly with the Aim-9J missile selected. If you are on a air-to-ground sortie, you only need to call up your bombs or Maverick missiles just prior to employing them. After attacking a ground target, re-select the Sidewinder mode. With the Sidewinder selected you will get the aspect caret presented in the HUD and you will be able to fire at the MiG as soon as you get an in range (IN RNG) indication. To shoot the Sidewinder follow these steps:

1. Select the missile.

2. Fly the target into the HUD. (The target does not need to be in the Missile Reticle.)

3. Keep the target in the HUD and wait for a flashing diamond in the HUD and an in range (IN RNG) indication.

4. Note the target line of sight (LOS) rate. The line of sight rate is the speed at which the target is moving across your HUD. If the target moves out of your HUD in the time it takes the missile to get there, the LOS may be too high for a good shot. The Sidewinder missile in Falcon usually takes about four to seven seconds to reach the target. If you can't keep the target in your HUD for that long, you will probably waste a missile if you shoot.

5. Shoot as soon as the above conditions are met!

The *J* model Sidewinder is a "back shooting" weapon. It is best to get behind the bandit before firing. The *L* model will let you shoot from all target aspects and is generally better against a hard-maneuvering target.

THE GUN

When the bandit is in close and is flashing back and forth across your HUD, draw your gun. The gun is used when the "stress factor" is up and the chips are down. The gun is an all-aspect weapon that can be fired when you are in tight on the bandit and inside missile parameters. If the LOS rate is high (as defined in the previous section) you should switch to guns. The following steps will help you kill the MiG with the gun.

1. Select the gun.

2. Observe the movement of the MiG and fly your jet to get your LCOS Pipper moving toward the bandit.

3. Prior to the bandit reaching the LCOS Pipper, open fire. Remember that the gun shoots unguided projectiles with a specific time of flight. Because of this, you must hold the target steady under the LCOS Pipper for bullet time of flight, or you must open fire early and keep firing until you get the LCOS Pipper over the target.

4. Since you have a very large load of 20-mm cannon shells in Falcon, shoot whenever the MiG gets close to your HUD.

WHY FIGHTER
PILOTS WERE BORN

Flying BFM in the F-16 is a wonderful thing. The F-16 is a small, highly maneuverable fighter that can dominate most other jets in a maneuvering fight. You must be aware, however, that maneuvering at high *G*s to get to the bandit's six o'clock is not the objective of the fight. Fighter pilots were born for one thing: to kill the enemy and survive the engagement. To kill the enemy you must use your weapons. The best air-to-air engagements are brutal ambushes of the enemy. One minute the bandit is flying along nice and relaxed, the next minute your missile hits him and his body parts are flying formation with pieces of his jet. Entering a sustained maneuvering fight can be very unhealthy in modern aerial combat. As you go around and around with the bandit, other pilots are attracted to the fight like moths to a flame. You may be winning the fight that you're aware of, while you're losing a fight that you don't know you're in. For this reason you should shoot every time you get in parameters on the enemy and end the fight quickly. The life you save will be your own.

AIR-TO-GROUND COMBAT 7

*"You can shoot down every MiG in the sky, but
if the tank commander of the lead Soviet tank
is eating lunch in your squadron when you
land, you've lost the war."*

— anonymous fighter pilot

It was the first Operational Readiness Inspection (ORI) for an overseas F-16 Wing and the "Wolf Pack" (the Eighth Tactical Fighter Wing) was tasked by the inspection team to mobilize for "war." An ORI is a fun-filled affair that usually lasts about one week and features all of the thrills and excitement of real war, including wearing full anti-chemical gear, flak vests, and steel helmets. You haven't experienced fun until you've tried to brief a complex mission while wearing a gas mask to a room full of pilots also wearing gas masks. Nobody can understand what you are saying; you shout, grunt, and hope for the best.

During an ORI you experience constant enemy attacks carried out by "sappers" and "enemy aircraft" that make you stop what you're doing, don all that stylish war apparel, and run for cover. Fighter pilots are issued .38 caliber pistols without bullets. In a real war they would presumably give you bullets—not that they would do any good against a very skilled and suicidal enemy soldier with an assault rifle.

In addition to the misery of life in and around the squadron during an ORI, you fly realistic "combat missions" that test the Wing's ability to carry out its wartime tasking. The Eighth Tactical Fighter Wing is stationed at Kunsan Air Base in the Republic of Korea, and has the primary mission of attacking the enemy in depth, disrupting and destroying their forces in the air and on the ground. The Wing flies at a grueling pace during

145

one of these inspections, which tests the stamina of both the pilots and the maintenance personnel. After experiencing an ORI as a young fighter pilot one quickly realizes that the fun has gone out of war fighting.

This was my second ORI. I had participated in my first at Clark Air Base in the Philippines while flying the F-4. In the Philippines I was a brand-new Lieutenant when the inspection hit the base. All I had to do was stay close to my leader and not do anything stupid. In the second ORI, I was a new Captain and a flight lead with about 600 total fighter hours, 500 in the F-4 and 100 in the F-16. At this stage in a fighter pilot's career it's normal to have a somewhat distorted view of yourself and your abilities. I felt omniscient and invulnerable and couldn't wait to take on the entire Soviet Air Force. The humbling experience of the USAF Fighter Weapons School was still in my future. Of course in reality I was no "Steve Canyon," and the first mission of the first overseas F-16 ORI proved it.

The afternoon the ORI inspectors showed up on the base, they handed us the Air Tasking Orders (ATO), which listed the missions we were going to fly the next day. The first mission of the "war" was a 12-aircraft raid on the island of Torishima off the coast of Okinawa, 500 miles to the south of Kunsan Air Base. The Wing Commander tasked our squadron to lead the raid, and my Squadron Operations Officer came and "asked" me if I could hack it. As he explained the mission to me, the words of a fighter pilot song came to mind: "I told him I would go, because they haven't found / A target in hell, that I couldn't pound." I answered, "This mission is no hill for a climber, sir. I thought for a minute there that you had something challenging for me." With those words the planning for the great raid on Torishima got under way.

It was after 8:00 P.M. by the time the ATO got sorted out. I started the detailed planning for the attack. The jets were armed with live Mk-84 2000lb bombs, and we had a prestrike and poststrike air refueling scheduled. After getting our prestrike fuel top-off, we were tasked to fly a 120 mile low-level that brought us to the target island. The island itself was just a rock out in the middle of the East China Sea with some vehicle hulks scattered around on it. I planned a low-level ingress (entrance to target area) and a fly-up to medium altitude with the four ships in trail formation. (*Ingressing* is a fighter pilot term that refers to entering enemy territory.) The threat was briefed as MiGs (played by F-15s), small arms fire, and AAA in the target area. All 12 pilots helped plan the mission, and by midnight we were ready for the 4:30 A.M. briefing. I stayed up until about 2:00 A.M. to double-check all of the numbers and make sure I had things straight in my head. The importance of the mission was underscored the next morning by the presence of the Wing Commander in the flight briefing. After the briefing we walked to our jets, and then took off into a clear and cold spring morning for what was supposed to be a three-hour mission.

We hit the tanker as scheduled, dropped off, and headed for the low-level start point. Everything looked fine as we descended to low altitude and started our run for the target. After about 60 miles we started to pick up a few clouds and had to fly lower to get under them. As we flew along, the clouds got thicker and the ceiling got lower. I switched to a ground map radar mode to examine the clouds, and discovered they were thunderstorms, very thick and dangerous. We were getting deeper and deeper into the storm at a low altitude, and I had to make a decision. I decided to weather-abort the mission. The 12-ship formation was strung out for about 20 miles on the low-level, so I figured each four-ship formation would turn around and return to the tanker track to get gas, and then we would reassess the situation.

As we began to turn around, my number four man had an electrical problem. Electrical problems in the F-16 can be serious, so I had my number three man escort him to the nearest airfield, which was Kadena Air Base in Okinawa, less than 150 miles to the southeast. They left the formation as we climbed to medium altitude. It was down to just me and the ORI inspector in my formation as we headed back to the tanker. I expected to see eight F-16s at the tanker track but there were only four of them. I asked the flight lead of the fourth ship where the other jets had gone and he said the others had had enough gas to make it all the way back to Kunsan and didn't need to air refuel. Now we were down to six jets from our original 12, and we still had our bombs loaded. So far this flight was definitely not one to write home about. As I was getting gas from the tanker I thought of a plan to try to hit the target with what was left of the strike package. Since we were fewer in number the tanker had more gas to give each aircraft. I asked the tanker to call his command post to see if he could stay in the refueling track another two hours so we could try another approach to the target. The tanker pilot made the call and said he would stay as long as we needed him. After all six jets got their fuel, I briefed a new plan. This time instead of flying the low-level we would try to fly around the storm line at medium altitude, keeping a close eye on our fuel.

Back at the "war" at Kunsan, the Wing Commander was informed that two aircraft with live bombs had just landed at Kadena AB. Shortly after he was told that a flight of four F-16s from the Torishima raid had just landed with *their* bombs still loaded about an hour and a half before the scheduled landing time. He immediately called the Supervisor of Flying (SOF), the guy who keeps track of airborne jets, and said, "What the hell is going here? Where are the other F-16s, and, specifically, where's the leader?" The SOF could only shrug his shoulders and say, "I don't know sir." It sure looked bad for the home team at this point; four jets on the ground back at the base with their bombs unexpended, two jets 500 miles away in Okinawa on the ground with unexpended bombs, and six jets unaccounted for somewhere over the East China Sea.

Meanwhile, our remaining six jets had finally beaten the weather by flying about 175 miles out of the way. We soon found the island and pounded the target with our Mk-84s, 45 minutes after our scheduled Time on Target (TOT). After hitting the target, we followed the same path back to the tanker, refueled, and flew home. When I got within 100 miles of Kunsan I called back with an in-flight report that the target was destroyed. We landed five hours after takeoff (instead of three hours as planned). I went back to the squadron and debriefed the Intelligence Officer and gathered up the rest of the flight (except for the guys in Okinawa). We finally pieced together that "goat rope" of a mission, and everyone scattered to fly other missions. Not much was said to me about the whole thing, and the Wing decided to downplay the raid and see what the inspector who flew on the mission reported. At the end of the week, the ORI ended, and we received the customary ORI debrief from the inspection team. They rated the raid on Torishima a success, despite the somewhat unorthodox execution of the mission. There is no doubt that I lost some style points, but the inspector that flew with me on the mission said, "The bottom line on the Torishima raid was that the target was destroyed and that all of the jets returned safely."

After the debrief, everyone gathered in the bar for the post-ORI celebration. Soon after the party started a few guys got up and said that they had written a song about the Wing's most memorable experience during the ORI. It was sung to the tune of "Sink the Bismarck," and it was entitled "The Torishima Raiders." It is not in my best interests to reveal all of the words to this song; fighter pilots don't make up songs to flatter anybody, and this song was no exception to that rule. I will give you the first few lines, which went something like this:

It was March of 1982 and the Wolf Pack got the task,
A raid on Torishima was all the inspectors asked,
Attack Torishima, that was the battle sound,
But the TOT came and went, and the Wolf Pack
    was nowhere to be found,

Well, as the saying goes, live and learn. On the Torishima raid I overreacted to the weather and almost lost sight of the reason I'd strapped into the jet that morning. There are only two objectives when you go out to beat mud (fly a ground-attack mission): destroy the target and survive to fight another day. Everything you do during that mission should move you closer to those two objectives.

This chapter will give you basic air-to-ground techniques that will help you achieve the fundamental objectives of the Falcon air-to-ground missions. It does not contain all of the answers, however; you will still have to learn from your own mistakes just as all the other fighter pilots do.

FALCON AIR-TO-GROUND FUNDAMENTALS

Aircraft cannot hold and control territory on the ground. This job is done primarily by a soldier on land with an M-16. The fighter pilot is always aware of that soldier and knows that he and the soldier are both part of an orchestrated air and land battle with the ultimate goal of defending or capturing ground objectives. Every war fought with aircraft has proven that air superiority is the most important mission flown by tactical aircraft. Without air superiority you cannot perform other vital missions such as ground attack, reconnaissance, and air resupply. While air superiority is a prerequisite to victory on the ground, it in itself does not guarantee victory. The modern battlefield is dominated by weapon systems such as tanks and aircraft with incredible mobility and firepower. Nevertheless, the outcome of the battle still rests primarily on the shoulders of the infantrymen. At some point, if the air battle is successful, the F-16 weapon system will be utilized in support of these men on the ground, and at this point the F-16 will start "beating mud" and "moving dirt" to accomplish this mission.

Attacking ground targets is fundamentally the same as attacking aircraft except that ground targets don't move as quickly and the attack geometry is far easier to understand. We will discuss techniques for employing three categories of air-to-ground weapons in Falcon: the point-and-shoot weapon, the free-fall bomb, and the guided missile. All of these weapons are delivered from a diving attack.

Strafing

The 20-mm gun is a point-and-shoot weapon that is very straightforward in Falcon. At the end of Chapter 4 we discussed the associated HUD symbology for strafe and how to call up the gun for an air-to-ground attack. This section will cover the tactical use of the gun.

The 20-mm gun in the Falcon simulation is a great weapon to use when you are in tight on a target and you don't have time to set up the attack. The other Falcon air-to-ground weapons take a lot more time and distance to employ. With the gun you can quickly call it up, point at the target, and shoot. The bullets fly out the gun barrel and head straight for where you pointed them. When things are happening too fast and you can't get lined up for a bomb or missile attack, draw your gun and execute the following steps:

1. Select the air-to-ground Strafe mode.

2. When the target comes into view, fly the jet so as to place your Flight Path Marker below the target, as shown in Figure 7-1.

Note: You're thinking, "Why don't I just aim at the target?" It is easier to aim the gun if you place the jet on a flight path below the target and fly

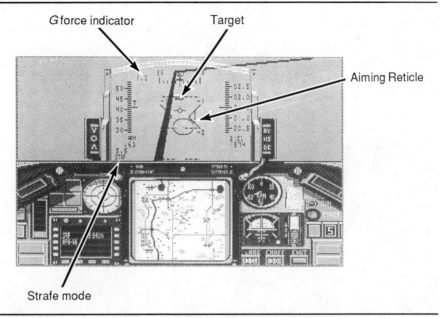

G force indicator   Target

Aiming Reticle

Strafe mode

Figure 7-1.   Initial Flight Path Market position for strafe

the Aiming Reticle up to the target. There are two reasons why aiming below the target makes strafing easier. First, as you start to bring your Aiming Reticle up to the target and concentrate on shooting, you will shallow out your dive angle instead of getting steeper. This is important because the steeper your dive at the target, the more altitude you will need to pull out without hitting the ground. If you initially point your Flight Path Marker above the target, you will have to dive more steeply while you are aiming and shooting. This could easily put you in a bad position in relation to the ground (too steep and too low).

The other reason not to point above the target applies mainly to the real F-16. If you point above the target you will have to push negative Gs to line up with it, and that is very uncomfortable when flying low to the ground on a strafing run. Negative Gs feel like going downhill on a rollercoaster.

Aiming Reticle

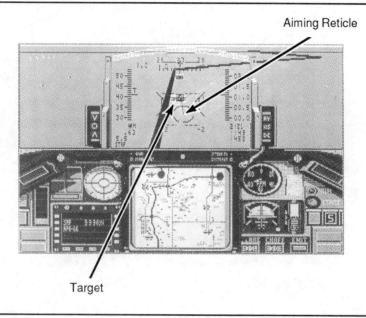

Target

Figure 7-2.   Aiming Reticle position for strafe

3. Fly the Aiming Reticle up to the target as shown in Figure 7-2, and hold it there.

4. Press the SPACEBAR once to lock-on to the target.

5. Open fire on the target by pressing the SPACEBAR a second time and holding it down as you keep the Aiming Reticle over the target.

6. After firing a two to three second burst, check your position in relation to the ground and think seriously about pulling up. Even if you are not close to the ground, you will have been flying a very predictable flight path for long enough. The Falcon POW camp is full of fighter pilots who flew a predictable flight path for too long.

Believe it or not, this really is an easy weapon to use once you get some practice. The key to strafing in Falcon is initially aiming below the target and then gradually pulling the Aiming Reticle up to cover the target.

Bombing

The free-fall bomb is the primary air-to-ground weapon used by aircraft throughout the world. In Falcon there are two types of free-fall bombs: the Mk-84 and the Durandel. This section will address employing these weapons in the simulation. Before we discuss actual techniques, there are a few things that the Falcon pilot should know about dropping bombs. Figure 7-3 shows a side view of the bombing triangle. This triangle shows the pilot the geometry of a bombing run and by so doing helps him visualize the mechanics of the attack. The diagram shows the following terms: *Aim-Off*

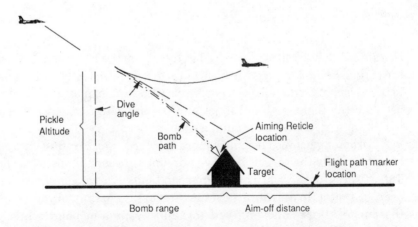

Figure 7-3. Side view of bombing triangle

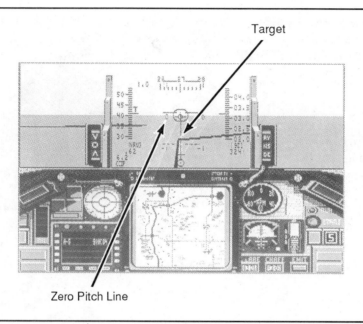

Target

Zero Pitch Line

Figure 7-4. Target position in the HUD prior to the bomb run

Distance is the distance, measured in feet, from the Flight Path Marker to the target. *Bomb Range* is the horizontal distance, in feet, from the aircraft to the target at bomb release. *Dive Angle* is the angle, measured in degrees, between the flight path of the jet and the horizon. *Pickle Altitude* is the height, in feet, above the ground at bomb release.

Dropping bombs is slightly more involved than strafing because you have to overfly the target in a dive and line up your aiming symbology in order to accurately drop a bomb. You can't make corrections once you pass over the target. In a strafe attack the target stays in front of your jet during the entire attack, allowing you to adjust your aim point while you're shooting. We have already discussed the Falcon CCIP HUD bombing symbology in Chapter 4. The next section will cover how to use the CCIP bomb symbology to accurately deliver the Mk-84 and Durandel.

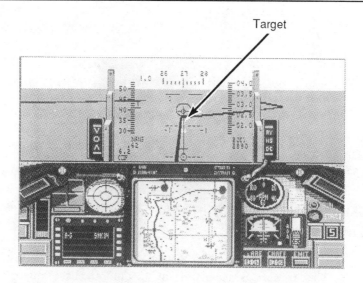

Target

Figure 7-5.   Target position in the HUD during bomb run

1. Select the desired free-fall weapon (Mk-84 or Durandel).

2. Fly straight at the target at 2,000 to 4,000 feet above the ground.

3. Note the position of the target in your HUD in relation to the Pitch
    Lines. When the target is between 5-20 degrees below the 0 Pitch
    Line, start your attack. Figure 7-4 shows the target in the correct
    position in the Falcon HUD.

4. Start the attack by flying your Flight Path Marker above the
    target, and put the target one third of the way down the CCIP
    bomb fall line as depicted in Figure 7-5.

Note: You must aim above the target with your Flight Path Marker
and achieve some aim-off distance or you will plant your rear end short of

the target without ever getting the Aiming Reticle over it. Plowing into the ground in this manner lacks style and is very unhealthy.

5. Hold the Flight Path Marker steady in relation to the target and adjust the flight path of your jet to keep the bomb fall line through the target. Remember that the bomb fall line shows the future path of the Aiming Reticle.

Note: This is the point in the bomb run when you must ask yourself the crucial question: "by the time my Aiming Reticle gets to the target, will my pickle altitude be high enough to allow me to pull out of this dive?" A good way to know the answer is to watch the "break X" symbol in the HUD. If the answer is yes, go on to step 6. If at any time in your approach to the target you see a big X in your HUD, then the answer to this question is no. Pull up out of the dive and pickle as the target goes through the Aiming Reticle. This is not an accurate way to deliver the bombs because the Aiming Reticle will pass through the target very quickly, giving you only a split second to pickle. However, in this situation it is a good idea to trade bomb accuracy for survival.

6. Watch the Aiming Reticle track up to the target and when it intersects the target, hit the SPACEBAR to pickle (release) the bomb. Figure 7-6 shows the Aiming Reticle over the target at release.

7. If the Delay cue is present after pickle, you must continue your approach to the target until you see "Rel" (release) in the HUD. The release symbol signals that the bombs are on their way to beat mud (and with any luck destroy the target).

8. After bomb release pull up and get away from the target. If you want to check and see where your bombs hit the ground, pull up into a 40-60 degree climb and press the **5** key to look directly behind you. With some practice you can use this technique to check the accuracy of your bomb deliveries. Be careful, though,

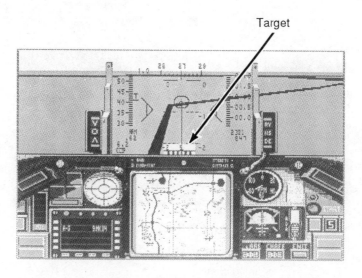

Target

Figure 7-6. Aiming Reticle position at bomb release

of putting on this type of air show at the higher levels of the game. The enemy will more than likely show their appreciation of your acrobatics over the target area by presenting you with your very own Surface-to-Air Missile.

Maverick Attack

The Maverick is a guided missile that requires the pilot only to lock-on to the target and launch the missile. It's employment is similar to strafing because you must point directly at the target in order to fire it. Once the missile is fired, the pilot can maneuver the jet freely and does not need to keep flying toward the target. The following steps will help you kill targets with the Maverick missile.

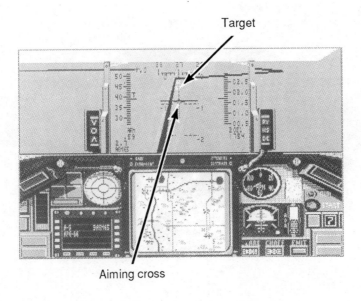

Target

Aiming cross

Figure 7-7.   Maverick Aiming Cross position at the start of attack

1. Select the Maverick.

2. Roll in on the target and place the Maverick Aiming Cross below the target as shown in Figure 7-7. The reason for this is the same as it was in strafing. It is easier to fly the Aiming Cross up to the target after you stabilize the jet on the attack, rather than trying to point directly at the target as you are maneuvering to attack.

3. Fly the Aiming Cross up to the target.

4. Press the **Q** key to get a view from the seeker head of the Maverick and use this view to fly and aim at the target.

5. Hit the SPACEBAR once to lock-on. If you have lock-on to the desired target, hit the SPACEBAR again to launch the missile. If you do not get a lock-on to the correct target hit the **X** key to break lock and reinitialize the Maverick, and then give it another try.

6. Once you launch the missile, press the **3** key to get out of the missile view and back into normal HUD view and then turn away from the target area.

7. As you are *egressing* (exiting the target area) press the **Q** key again to watch the missile impact the target. If you are not in a high threat situation, you can switch back to a normal HUD view after step 5 and watch the Maverick fly to the target. The problem with this technique is that your flight path is predictable for a long period of time.

The Maverick missile is the best weapon to use in a high threat environment in Falcon because you do not have to get as close to the target as you do when dropping the Mk-84 and Durandel. In addition, it is easier to assess the results of your attack.

SAM THREAT REACTION

There are three types of SAMs in the Falcon simulation: the radar-guided SA-2 and SA-6 and the IR-guided SA-7. This section will give you a few survival techniques for your bag of tricks. When the SAMs start flying, there are no surefire ways of avoiding or defeating them. If you want to be completely safe, don't take off in the first place. At some point, the cause of freedom will require the fighter pilot to go in harm's way.

Using the Threat Indicator

In Falcon the only dependable way to tell if you have been engaged by a SAM is by checking your Threat Warning Indicator. This gauge will give you an audio and visual signal for radar SAM lock-on and launch. For IR SAMs you will only get a launch indication because the SA-7 does not have radar associated with it. Reacting to SAMs is similar to the defensive BFM procedures that we covered in Chapter 6. A minimum amount of creative thinking is required when you become engaged by a SAM. What is required by the fighter pilot is reaction. Unfortunately, in air combat quickly reacting the wrong way won't work. What will work is executing a sound game plan quickly and correctly as soon as you become engaged by a SAM.

The steps discussed shortly outline a game plan that will help keep you alive when your jet turns into a SAM magnet. All of these steps are based on you detecting a SAM in your Threat Indicator. If you do not detect a SAM launch with your Threat Indicator then you are bound for the meat locker and the following procedure won't help you.

Missile Lock-On Indication

When engaged by the SA-2 or SA-6 you should get a lock-on indication in the Threat Indicator. This indication will appear as a "LCK" on the panel to the left of the circular scope on the Threat Indicator. (If you need a review of what this looks like reference Chapter 5). In addition to this visual display you will also get an audio indication of radar lock-on that consists of a beeping sound. Don't worry about which type of radar missile is locking-on to you because you can't tell, and it doesn't matter anyway; dying is dying regardless of missile type. What is important is that you execute the following steps as soon as you get a SAM lock-on indication:

1. Turn on your ALQ-131 jamming pod immediately by pressing the E key. If you don't have a jamming pod loaded, you'd better hope the following steps work.

2. Dispense chaff by pressing the DEL key.

3. Descend to lower altitude and go to AB as fast as you can.

In Falcon it is a good idea to get down to 500 feet to avoid radar-guided threats. If the lock-on indication goes away turn off your jamming pod and continue with your mission. Be ready to repeat the steps if a SAM locks you up again. If you do not break the lock-on of the SAM, keep flying fast and low, with your jamming pod on, and keep dispensing chaff.

Missile Launch Indication

If a lock-on indication turns into a missile launch indication, you are very close to getting morted. Again, don't worry about what type of missile is being fired at you. Execute as many of the following steps as you need to avoid the SAM. After a SAM launch at your jet, you have the rest of your life to react correctly. Remember to dispense both chaff and flares *throughout* the following steps:

1. Check your jamming pod to ensure that it is on (if you have one loaded).

2. If at medium altitude, perform a slicing maneuver at high *G* to low altitude. Figure 7-8 show a cockpit view of this maneuver. Be careful you don't double dribble yourself off the ground. If you are at low altitude perform a hard *G* turn with at least 90 degrees of heading change.

3. If you are still alive, get ready for the next missile by going as fast as you can and getting lower if you are not already on the deck.

The primary thing to remember during a SAM launch is that you must use *all* of your ECM, and put high *G*s on the jet. It is very difficult to actually see a SAM coming at you in Falcon so don't base your SAM defensive game plan on picking up the missile visually and then reacting. If you do, you will begin your defensive reactions just about the time the missile is exploding.

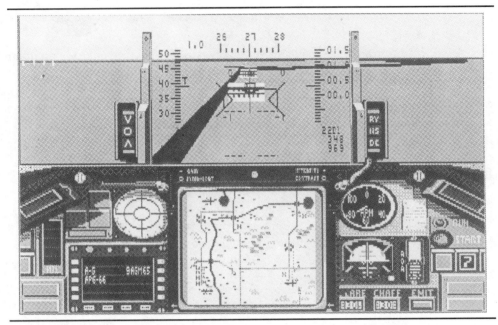

Figure 7-8.   Slice-to-low altitude

Ejection

If you do everything correctly and still get hit by a SAM, it's time to ride the old nylon elevator down to mother earth. When you can no longer control the jet due to battle damage, press CTRL-E to bail out. Once you have lost control of the aircraft do not delay ejecting.

MOVING EARTH

There is no doubt that moving the mud with bombs is a thankless job. The guys that fly the air-to-ground sorties do most of the dying and get a lot less recognition than the guys flying air-to- air. Despite this fact, destroying ground targets with fighter aircraft is an essential part of the war effort. When the enemy parks tanks on your airfield, you really have lost the war. The next chapter will lead you through planning a mission and will discuss the tactical considerations of a Falcon ground-attack mission. Somebody has got to stop the commie war machine, and that somebody is you.

Falcon Tactics

8

Knowing how to fight the MiG one-on-one or how to drop a bomb on a target does not necessarily mean success in the Falcon simulation. These and the other techniques that we have discussed so far are just basic skills. Now that you have learned these skills we can move on to a discussion of employing your jet in the Falcon tactical environment. In this chapter we will tie together all of the basics, describe some advanced techniques, and teach you to plan and fly a mission in the simulation.

THE TACTICAL ENVIRONMENT

The tactical environment consists of the air and land battle area and the disposition of friendly and enemy forces within this area. The enemy's capabilities, the Falcon's capabilities, and the terrain all make up the tactical environment. In the Falcon simulation this environment changes as you change the level of the game. Moving from Lieutenant to Colonel changes both the threat and the abilities of your jet but does not change the steps that you take to plan and execute a mission.

165

The Enemy

The enemy has the single biggest impact on your ability to execute your mission. If there were no enemy presence on the battlefield, there would be no need for tactics. You would just fly along at about 5,000-10,000 feet, circle around the target until you were perfectly lined up, and then bomb it from an altitude that would give you the exact impact angle on the bomb that you desired. We all know from playing the game that this approach won't work. Every target in Falcon that is worth bombing is defended by the enemy. Our mission plan will have to take this threat into account or we will end up wearing a lot of enemy missiles before we even get close to the target area.

What You Know

The tactical plan that you will use in Falcon will be built almost entirely around what you know about the position of the enemy threat systems. In Falcon, the SA-2 and SA-6 SAMs are positioned at fixed sites, which do not change. Before flying a mission, you should note the location of these systems by checking your COMED map or by using the map in Appendix A of this text. With this information you can construct your game plan to avoid flying near the sites whenever possible. Later in this chapter we will discuss how to accomplish this task.

The range of the SA-2 missile is about 30 miles in Falcon and the range of the SA-6 is about 37 miles when the Falcon is flying at medium altitude. At low altitude the range of these SAMs is sharply reduced and their performance is severely degraded. Since the dimensions of the entire battle area in Falcon are approximately 40 miles wide by 40 miles long you are in the envelope of both of these SAMs immediately after takeoff if you climb to medium altitude. The best way to avoid getting hosed by an SA-2 or by an SA-6 is to get low and stay low when you are within 15 miles of the SAM site.

Again, most of your mission planning will center around avoiding SA-2 and SA-6 sites since their positions are known and accurately depicted on your COMED map. Figure 8-1 shows an expanded view of the Falcon COMED and the position of the fixed SAMs.

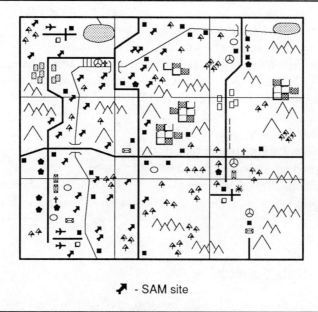

↗ - SAM site

Figure 8-1.   COMED map of SAM site positions

What You Don't Know

The saying "what you don't know can't hurt you" may be true concerning matters of the heart, but in combat what you don't know will kill you. Unfortunately when it comes to combat there are quite a large number of unknowns. In Falcon, one of the biggest unknowns is the SA-7. The SA-7 is a highly mobile SAM that is carried and fired by enemy soldiers. You do not know the position of every individual, enemy of freedom running around the battlefield, so you can't know the positions of the SA-7s. The SA-7 is a small SAM and in Falcon it has a range of about six miles. You can avoid it entirely by either flying above 10,000 feet or flying very low and fast. Speeds over 500 knots and altitudes of less than 1,000 feet give the missile real problems. High altitude flying works best but you must determine the position of the fixed SAMs (SA-2 and SA-6) and their range before you start driving the Falcon around above 10,000 feet.

Another very dangerous unknown is the position of the enemy MiGs. Aircraft are not fixed in a specific location and are highly mobile and flexible in their engagement doctrine. They may lie in wait over enemy lines, or they may cross into friendly territory and attack you over your own airfield. The good news, in Falcon, is that you will only have to deal with one of these threat categories (MiGs or SAMs) at a time, and you can make this work to your advantage. In addition your Falcon has excellent sensors to detect attacking MiGs.

One warning about MiGs in the Falcon simulation: if you have your pod turned on and you are not being engaged by SAMs, a MiG will home in on your pod transmissions almost every time. For this reason only turn the pod on when your Threat Indicator shows enemy missile lock-on or launch.

Falcon Capabilities

The Falcon does not enter the tactical environment defenseless. The jet is well equipped to destroy the enemy and survive to fight another day. The primary Falcon tools for achieving success in combat are weapons, countermeasures, and maneuver.

Weapons

When you build your tactical plan for destroying the target you must think carefully about your choice of weapons. The primary consideration is the probability that the chosen weapon will destroy the target. For example, there is no need to shoot Mavericks at a runway because they will not damage this type of target. When several weapons can be used to destroy a target, you must consider how easy the weapon is to employ and how much exposure you will have to any danger during weapon delivery.

Countermeasures

The Falcon has three basic countermeasure systems: chaff, flares, and the jamming pod. These systems can greatly impact your ability to accomplish the mission but you must keep in mind that these are defensive systems and as such are of limited value. The best way to deal with the enemy is to attack and destroy him. Unfortunately in Falcon you are not armed with offensive stand-off weapons that can be used against SAMs. We have already discussed in detail how to use your chaff, flares, and pod. Use these systems when you become engaged by the enemy but do not count on their defeating the enemy. The best way to survive the air battle in Falcon is to build a mission plan that avoids as much as the known threat as possible.

Maneuver

The maneuverability of the Falcon is one of your biggest advantages against the enemy threat systems. High *G* maneuvering, in combination with countermeasures, makes you a very difficult target to kill. Remember, you must be close to 450 knots in order for your turns to be effective against SAMs or MiGs. Any faster or slower and you will not be able to turn fast or tight enough. Use the throttle and speed brakes as necessary to achieve the proper airspeed once you start maneuvering.

Terrain

The Falcon battle area has natural terrain and cultural features that the fighter pilot must be aware of. Mountains, buildings, and roads are the primary features that will affect your mission planning and execution.

Mountains can be used to mask your approach to the target. Whenever possible keep the mountains between your jet and the known SAM sites to shield your approach. If a SAM locks-on to your aircraft, you may be able to duck behind a mountain to break missile line of sight. *Line of sight* is simply the ability of the missile or missile launch site to maintain a direct view of your jet. If you break this direct view by putting a mountain between your jet and their position, you will break line of sight and they will not be able to engage your aircraft. Line of sight must be maintained by the SAMs in Falcon in order for them to guide on your jet.

Another factor that affects line of sight is the curvature of the earth. Figure 8-2 shows the effect of the curvature of the earth and the altitude of your jet to line of sight. If you fly below 500 feet, the SAM sites will not

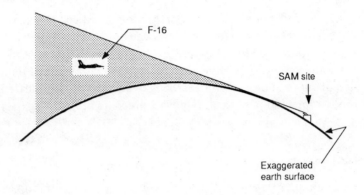

Figure 8-2.   Curvature of earth effecting line of sight

pick up your jet until you are inside 20 miles. Mountains and the curved surface of the earth can be used to delay the enemy's detection of your jet.

Roads and buildings are the next important terrain features to consider in your mission plan and execution. Roads are man-made lines of communication that should be avoided whenever possible. They are easy to see from the air so there is a natural tendency for pilots to follow them. Remember that the enemy is conducting a battle and is moving troops and material on these roads. The combat assets that the enemy moves along the roads will be defended by SA-7s, so heads up. At some point in your mission you will have to fly over a road in enemy territory. When you have to fly over a road, cross it as quickly as possible. If you have to fly parallel to a road, offset your flight path five-ten miles to avoid unwanted attention from possible traffic on the road. The last thing to remember about roads is that they are only *potential* threat areas. You would rather fly near a road in enemy territory than a known SAM site.

Buildings should be avoided for the same reasons that you avoid roads. The enemy tends to congregate in cities and towns, and has some stake in defending these areas. Fly around buildings whenever possible to avoid a possible SA-7 threat. Keep in mind that the SA-7 can be encountered anywhere in enemy territory, but you are most likely to encounter this SAM near man-made terrain features.

MISSION PLANNING

The key to formulating a successful plan is understanding the mission objective and your capabilities compared to the known and expected enemy threats. The mission objective is to destroy an enemy ground or air target and survive. In order to do this you must minimize your exposure to the enemy threat systems and fly an attack that will give you a reasonable chance of success. The probability of killing the target must be carefully weighed against the probability of your jet being shot down; any plan you devise should balance these two factors.

The Target

Mission Planning starts at the target. Each Falcon mission has a target that must be destroyed. Start by checking the target and deciding what type of weapons to use in destroying it. The following is a list of targets and the best weapons to employ against them.

SAM Sites

AGM-65 Maverick missile

20-mm strafe

Mk-84 2000lb bomb

SAM sites are soft targets and easy to destroy if you survive long enough to get your weapons off the jet. You should never duke it out with a SAM site unless it is absolutely necessary (such as when your target is a SAM site or right next to a SAM site). The Maverick is the best weapon because it will allow you to stand off from the target, improving your chance of survival. Strafe is the next choice for the same reason. The Mk-84 is a very effective weapon against a SAM site but requires you to overfly the target area.

There is one important piece of information that you should know before you try the old "Mat Dillon" routine with your Maverick against a SAM site—a Surface-to-Air Missile is a lot faster than your Maverick. Shortly after you both "draw" your weapons and fire, the enemy's missile will be in the vicinity of your pink body getting ready to go boom, while your missile will still be chugging along, still several seconds from impact. Again, if the mission calls for destroying SAM sites then you have no choice, but remember that not many fighter pilots who attack SAM sites for sport are still around.

Buildings (Including Barracks, Hangars, and Power Stations)

AGM-65 Maverick missile

Mk-84 2000lb bomb

The Maverick is again the weapon of choice because of its stand-off capability. Mk-84s are actually better weapons against these types of targets due to the bigger blast and fragmentation effects that you get from a large bomb. Again, aircraft survival plays a large part in the choice of weapon.

Tanks

AGM-65 Maverick missile

Mk-84 2000lb bomb

The Maverick missile was invented to replace bombs in the role of killing tanks so Mavericks are by far the best choice when attacking tanks. Use the bomb only if you can't use the Maverick.

Bridges

Mk-84 2000lb bomb

AGM-65 Maverick missile

The best weapon against a bridge is a bomb. The Maverick missile allows you to stand off but it shouldn't be your first weapon choice because it is a relatively small warhead with a tendency to miss bridges. If you miss the target you will have to re-attack, so you are better off using a bomb and reducing your long-term exposure to the threat.

Runways

Durandal Anti-Runway bomb

In the Falcon simulation this is the only effective weapon against runways.

Parked Aircraft

AGM-65 Maverick missile

20-mm strafe

Either one of these weapons will be effective against this soft target. Keep in mind, however, that you must stand off as much as possible to minimize your exposure to the threat; the Maverick is your best stand-off weapon.

The Threat Picture

After selecting your weapons, look at the known threats that lie between your airfield and the target area. In addition to SAM sites, watch for roads and buildings that may be a factor in plotting the mission.

Attack Plan

It is now time to build your attack plan. There is a saying about fighter mission planning: Measure it with a micrometer, mark it with chalk, and cut it with an ax. This means that the planning is done in great detail but the execution of the plan is not very precise. The reason for this is, of course, the dynamic nature of the tactical environment. You should still take the time necessary to construct a good plan. Just remember that things seldom go according to plan once the shooting starts.

Ingressing

Remember that ingressing refers to entering enemy territory and approaching the target. To pick your ingress route you should analyze the following factors:

- Position of known enemy SAM sites.

- Positions of mountains that can be used to mask your jet.

- Buildings and roads that may be possible SA-7 sites.

- Altitude of your ingress and its effects on the known and expected SAMs.

- Speed of your ingress and its effect on your exposure to the enemy. Another fighter pilot saying is "speed is life." This is true but must be weighed against fuel consumption. If you drive around in AB for too long and suck the Falcon fuel tank dry, you'll discover that a flamed-out F-16 flies like a LA-Z-Boy recliner.

- How much gas will you need for the mission? In the Falcon simulation always take an external gas tank. You can never have too much fuel.

After considering all of these factors you can start to formulate a route into the target area. You will soon discover that you cannot avoid all of the enemy SAM systems and will have to fly near or over some of them in order to accomplish the mission. I have found that the best way to ingress the target area when you have to go within 15 miles of a SA-2 or SA-6 is at 500 feet or lower, flying 500 knots. Use the mountains to hide your jet as much as possible. This is not the only way to do it, but it seems to work best in most cases in Falcon when ingressing into the target area.

Weapons Delivery

The next thing to plan is your weapons delivery. To accomplish this, look at how the target is positioned and plan your attack to maximize your chances of destroying the target without getting yourself morted. Some simple rules of thumb will help you plan the correct axis of attack on a target in Falcon:

- When bombing bridges, make your attack down the length of the bridge. During your attack fly down the road approaching the bridge. This will give you a bigger target from six to twelve o'clock to the target where most Falcon bombing errors occur. When dropping bombs in Falcon, you have a tendency to miss the target by dropping either short or long.

   The same applies to a Durandal attack on a runway. Approach the runway in the same direction that you would fly if you were landing. Since there are no winds in the Falcon simulation, it is best to give yourself the biggest target in the area where you have the most error. If you had a cross wind, you would attack these targets from a different angle.

- When shooting a Maverick missile at a building in the Falcon simulation you should attack the building broadside to give the missile the biggest target possible.

- Always try to line up targets in Falcon so that you can take out more than one in a single pass. The enemy barracks in the Roach Motel mission or the aircraft on the runway in the Killer Bees mission are examples of targets that can be lined up.

- When in doubt about which direction to attack the target, come in from the most direct route that keeps you clear of the enemy.

Waypoints   *Waypoints,* or *destinations,* are coordinates for locations on the ground. The F-16 navigation computer constantly calculates the aircraft position over the ground using latitude and longitude grid coordinates. In the F-16, the pilot can type the latitude and longitude of the target into the computer and get heading and distance to the target displayed in the HUD. In Falcon, when you select a mission to fly, the latitude and longitude coordinates of the target for that mission is automatically loaded into the Falcon navigation "computer". For every mission in Falcon the waypoints for the target of interest will be loaded, and will display the pilot range to the target in the HUD. Figure 8-3 shows the Falcon HUD display and waypoint 6, which is labeled D6, in the HUD. Waypoint D6 is loaded

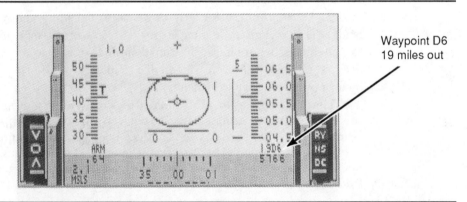

Figure 8-3.   Waypoint displayed in HUD

when you select the Roach Motel mission. Right beside the waypoint number is the range of the Falcon to the target in miles.

If you want to change the waypoint number (and the corresponding ranging information), press ; (semi-colon) to increase the waypoint number and ' (single quote) to decrease the waypoint number. Changing waypoints can be very useful. The best way to use this feature is to use the automatic range to your target for your attack. After the attack, decrement the waypoint to 0, by pressing ' (single quote) until you get to D0. D0 is the waypoint for your airfield so you now have a range read-out to the base presented in the HUD.

The Pop-Up Attack   The pop-up attack is used in Falcon when you approach the target from low altitude. You only need to execute a pop-up in Falcon in order to find the target and get lined up. A very low approach to the target will make target acquisition difficult and you may not see the target until you are in too close to make an attack. Popping-up from that low approach may help you get a Maverick shot off at longer range even when the target is easily seen because you will spot the target from farther away as you climb to higher altitude.

Execute the attack by approaching the target at low altitude (500 feet). When your range to the target is five miles (as shown by the waypoint display in your HUD) start a five degree climb as depicted in your HUD in Figure 8-4. Level off between 1,000-2,000 feet. When you see the target, line up and start your attack.

Egressing

A number of Falcon pilots carefully plan how to get into the target area but many of them forget to plan how they are going to get out. Fortunately in Falcon the best way in is also the best way out, and you can usually just reverse your course and fly back to the base. The same planning considerations apply to both ingressing and egressing the target area. Minimize your exposure to the threat by flying low and fast and using terrain where you can.

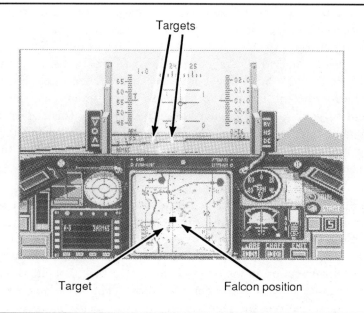

Figure 8-4. HUD showing 5° climb for pop-up attack

Emitters

When you plan your attack on the target you must also plan what to do with your emitters. An *emitter* is anything that gives off (emits) energy that can be used by the enemy to find and kill you. The Falcon radar and ALQ-119 jamming pod are the two emitters that must be factored into your mission planning. In the Falcon simulation you should keep both of these emitters off until they are needed when flying an air-to-ground mission. The jamming pod is toggled off and on with the **E** key and the radar can be turned off and on by pressing the **R** key.

The question that fighter pilots should ask when deciding on how to employ emitting sensors and countermeasures is "does the emitter do more for me than it does for the enemy?" If the answer to this is yes, then go ahead and turn the emitter on. When flying an air-to-ground mission in Falcon, I have found that the answer to this question is no, for both the radar and jamming pod, during the initial ingress into the target area. Once the SAMs find you (when you get a missile lock-on indication), turn your pod on. When you exit the target area and SAMs are no longer a factor, turn the pod off. Having the jamming pod on for too long is like painting "shoot me" on your jet. The radar should also be turned off as you ingress the target area until a MiG actually shows up on your Threat Indicator. When you start maneuvering to kill him, turn the radar back on. In an air-to-air mission turn the radar on and keep it on in order to find the MiGs.

Roach Motel

We will now go through an actual mission and apply the steps that we have already discussed. The mission is Roach Motel and the objective for this mission is to destroy two barrack buildings that are located to the west of our airfield near an east/west road. Figure 8-5 shows the location of the targets.

The Target

The first thing to do is select the appropriate weapon for this target. Mavericks are the first choice since the targets are buildings. Load your jet with as many Aim-9Ls as you can get, as well as three Maverick missiles, one fuel tank, and a jamming pod. There are only two buildings to destroy in the target area but even the great ones occasionally miss the target.

Threat Picture

Next, jump in the jet and start it up. In Falcon we do our mission planning sitting out at the end of the runway. Switch to the Map display on the COMED by pressing the **C** key. Examine the target area and the fixed

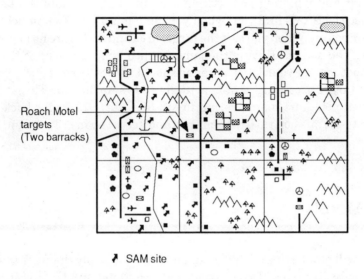

Roach Motel
targets
(Two barracks)

↗ SAM site

Figure 8-5. COMED map of threats and terrain features

SAMs, mountains, towns, and roads, all of which will affect your flight. Figure 8-5 shows these threats and terrain features.

Attack Plan

Now you must figure out how to get into enemy territory, destroy those barracks, and get out again. Figure 8-6 shows a planned route of flight after analyzing the threat and the terrain features. By noting the position of the fixed SAM sites and the terrain, we will fly a route that will take us in to the North after take-off and into the target area from the west. We don't want to go straight for the target because that path will take us down a major road in relatively flat terrain. Without mountain peaks to mask our approach we will be an easy target for the SAMs, and flying down a road means a potential SA-7 threat.

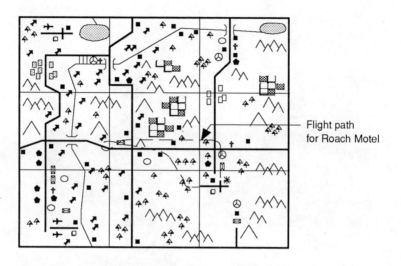

Figure 8-6.   Suggested ground track

There are several other routes we could take that would give us terrain masking opportunities, but we would have to fly a longer route that would increase our exposure to the threat. The longer it takes you to get to the target, the more time the enemy has to detect your presence and kill you. Remember, you must minimize your exposure to the threat in three ways: fly low, fast, and directly to the target allowing for the terrain and the position of any threat. The following section outlines one of many good options for attacking this target.

Route of Flight

Based on the position of the fixed SAM sites, go north (360 degrees) after takeoff to use the mountains west of the target to mask your approach. There is a prominent east/west road that you will cross as you fly north. The target barracks lie along the road, 20 miles to the west of our airfield.

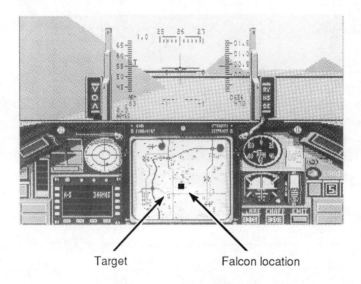

Target   Falcon location

Figure 8-7.   HUD viw of target ingress

After crossing the road turn west (270 degrees). On this heading you will soon approach two mountain peaks.

Fly this route at 500 feet and 500 knots using your Map display as a navigation aid. Have your Aim-9L selected and have your radar and pod turned off.

After getting around the first mountain peak start a turn toward the target area and call up the Maverick missile. Your range to the target at this point will be six to eight miles, which you can read in the lower-right corner of the HUD. Figure 8-7 shows a cockpit view of the attack at this point.

Keep on driving straight down and if you have not seen the target after four miles, start a pop-up maneuver and climb to 1,000-2,000 feet. When you do see the targets, concentrate on getting the Maverick missile locked-on, and fire when you get a good lock. After firing one missile don't get mesmerized by its movement. Line up the next target, lock-on, and fire.

After the second missile leaves the rail, break hard, and head back the way you came. You can select the view from the Maverick missile to assess your attack by pressing the **Q** key. Another way to check out the results of your attack is to keep flying toward the target and wait for your missiles to impact.

After the attack, egress by reversing the route you took into the target area. Go low and fast and call up your Aim-9L again for the return trip. Call up waypoint D0 (your airfield) in the HUD by pressing ' (single quote) until it counts down to 0. When you see that you are ten mile from the field, turn to line up and select the ILS mode by pressing F7. Slow down quickly to set up your landing pattern by pulling back the throttle and extending the speed brakes.

This is only one of several tactical plans for accomplishing the Roach Motel mission. The best plan is the one that works; you should use your imagination and the tactical principles outlined in this text to come up with your own plans.

The What Ifs

A good fighter pilot always mentally runs through the "what ifs" prior to takeoff. The kind of what ifs we need to look at in Falcon primarily involve the enemy. What if a MiG shows up on your Threat Indicator as you approach the target? What if a SAM fires at you during your attack? What if you are hit by an enemy missile and damaged prior to making your attack? There are literally dozens of what ifs that you must consider in Falcon. I can't give you the absolute correct course of action for all of these situations because there is no approved solution to a specific tactical situation. What works one day may not be as effective the next and almost every situation is unique in some way. I can give you some rules of thumb that will help you build a complete tactical perspective of the Falcon battle.

The first rule of thumb is *always react immediately* to a missile lock-on or launch no matter what you are doing.

Second, it is better for your longevity in Falcon to have a MiG around rather than SAMs. For this reason you should use the Threat Indicator to predict when a MiG becomes a dire threat and *then* react to him. (A threat becomes dire when the MiG locks-on you. When this occurs, engage and kill him using the excellent air-to-air instruction and penetrating insights provided in Chapter 6 of this text.) Until a MiG locks-on, you can keep pressing in to the target area.

Third, if you are hit by a missile and can still shoot your weapons and control your jet, attack the target if you are inside five miles. Outside this range, the chance of success is very poor. Always expect a MiG to show up at your home field when you are low on gas. A fighter pilot corollary to Murphy's Law says, "fuel need is inversely proportional to fuel in the jet." If this happens you have to defend yourself using the techniques we discussed in Chapter 6. There is no need to die with gas in the jet so defend yourself by flying the jet in Mil power and then try to make it to the field when you kill the MiG or escape it.

The last rule of thumb that will solve most of your what if questions is "think survival first, and target destruction second". This means that you should go after the target like John Wayne, but if things take a turn for the worse and you find yourself out of airspeed, fuel, and ideas, switch to another tactic and give peace a chance. Get out of there and go back when things are more in your favor.

None of the techniques and rules of thumb in this chapter, or anywhere else in the book for that matter, are etched in stone. The challenge in the Falcon simulation is to develop your own techniques and style based on your abilities and your perspective of the battle. A story from the book *Lucifer's Hammer* (Jerry Pournelle, Larry Niven [New York: Playboy Press, 1977]), comes to mind when speaking about flying in Falcon and life in general. In the book, a giant comet crashes into the earth somewhere in the Pacific Ocean. Several crazy surfers (fighter pilot types no doubt) realize that a very big tidal wave will crash into California, so they head for the beach to try and catch the wave. When the monstrous wave arrives, a few brave souls actually get up and ride it toward the shore. One surfer rides the wave for a long distance. Finally, a tall building looms in the distance, and he knows he will soon be smashed against it—but he rides on. "Death inevitable, but if death is inevitable what is left? Style, only style." No Falcon pilot will live forever in the simulation, so what's left is style. Do your best and fly the jet with style.

No Rules in a Knife Fight

"You are a warrior among men—now ply your spear and show yourself a warrior! Now let dreadful war be your heart's desire...."

—From Homer's *Iliad*
Translated by W.H.D. Rouse

Fighting in the air is a relatively new and unique form of warfare. The glamour of flight and the beauty and power of fighter planes have given air combat a special place in current history. The fighter pilot will continue to play an important part in shaping history but this role will one day pass away. During the next century, technology will overtake the fighter pilot and one-on-one dogfights in manned aircraft will be replaced by impersonal computer-chip combat between drones. This form of air warfare, however, is still in the future. For the present, the personal skill and courage of fighter pilots will determine the outcome of the war in the air.

Falcon helps you experience this form of combat but demands a price in return. The Falcon pilot must learn the fundamentals of air combat in order to experience a modern air battle. The more you learn about your jet and how to employ it in the simulation, the closer you will get to the feeling of real air combat.

THE INVISIBLE HAND

We have discussed a fighter pilot's perspective, covered the basics of flying the Falcon, and learned how to deal with the enemy in order to get a tactical perspective of air combat. The most important thing to learn now is how to bridge the gap between knowing what to do in a given situation and actually doing it.

The first part of the challenge is knowing what to do in the Falcon tactical environment. Hopefully you have gained some knowledge of air combat and can kill the enemy and survive using your own unique style. The combat situations presented in the simulation are dynamic and your response to each specific condition, whether successful or unsuccessful, gives you experience that builds your situation awareness. As you gain situation awareness you will learn how to react in increasingly complex situations.

The second half of the challenge is executing the correct course of action. For example, you may know that in a certain situation you need to turn the jet at high Gs, dispense chaff and flares, turn the pod on, and duck behind a mountain, but you may not have the "flying" skill necessary to pull all of this off. This is not unusual. There will be times in Falcon when your situation awareness is high, and you know precisely what to do but a big invisible hand emerges from your computer's disk drive and starts choking you just as you are about to execute the correct move. You will find yourself struggling in the grip of this hand, unable to lift a finger while a MiG presses in and sticks you with a missile. This happens to all fighter pilots, and the only way to keep this "hand" at bay is to gain experience. The more you fight, the smarter and more fluid you become as a fighter pilot.

CONCLUSION

There is nothing simple about air combat in the Falcon simulation. By now you have discovered that Falcon is complex and difficult to master. The

Falcon simulation re-creates the world of the fighter pilot, and in doing this creates a demand for the same air combat skills and knowledge that actual fighter pilots require.

The realism of this air combat simulation is not brought about entirely by constructing a precise physical model of reality. Falcon does mirror real-world air combat in many ways; however, the strength of the simulation lies primarily in re-creating the psychological environment of air combat. Flying and fighting in modern jet aircraft is as much a mental exercise as it is a physical activity. With the aid of this text, the simulation pilot can enter the "real" world of the fighter pilot. In this world the enemy threat is a powerful force that shapes your tactics and the outcome of the battle. You are in a fight where every action receives instant feedback in the form of victory or defeat. You must have confidence in your abilities and in your jet as you face numerous rapid-fire "life and death" decisions. You are a warrior in the world of Von Richthofen and Gabreski—flying and fighting in Falcon air combat.

MISSION MAPS

The two maps presented in this appendix will help you plan your missions. The maps point out the targets for specific missions, as well as natural and man-made landmarks, which you must consider in plotting your course.

If you are unsure about the navigating techniques that would allow you to use mountains to your advantage or to avoid man-made obstacles such as roads and buildings, review the "Terrain" section in Chapter 8.

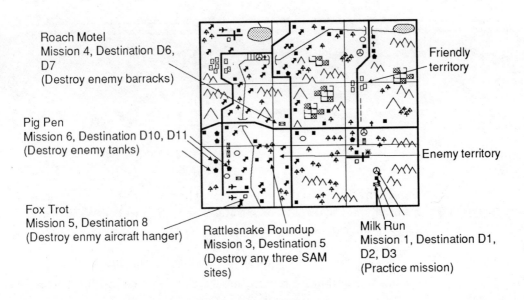

Black Bandit
Mission 2, Destination D4
(Shoot down one MiG)

Roach Motel
Mission 4, Destination D6,
D7
(Destroy enemy barracks)

Friendly
territory

Pig Pen
Mission 6, Destination D10, D11
(Destroy enemy tanks)

Enemy territory

Fox Trot
Mission 5, Destination 8
(Destroy enmy aircraft hanger)

Rattlesnake Roundup
Mission 3, Destination 5
(Destroy any three SAM
sites)

Milk Run
Mission 1, Destination D1,
D2, D3
(Practice mission)

Figure A-1. Mission map (mission 1 through mission 6)

Spark Plug
Mission 8, Destination D13
(Destroy enemy power plant)

Pay Back
Mission 9, Destination D14
(Destroy terrorist headquarters)

Killer Bees
Mission 11, Destination D17, D18
(Destroy enemy runway and aircraft)

Shopping Spree
Mission 7, Destination D12
(Destroy enemy communication
 center)

K.O.
Mission 12, Destination D19, D20
(Destroy enemy hanger, bridge, and
tank)

Double Dragon
Mission 10, Destination D15, D16
(Destroy enemy bridges)

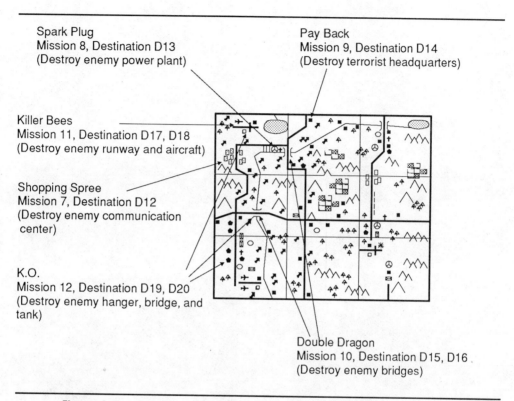

Figure A-2.   Mission map (mission 7 through mission 12)

Trademarks

Falcon™	Spectrum Holobyte
IBM® AT®	International Business Machines, Corp.
IBM® XT®	International Business Machines, Corp.
Macintosh™	Apple Computer, Inc.

Index

Keyboard Command Layout (IBM PC/AT)

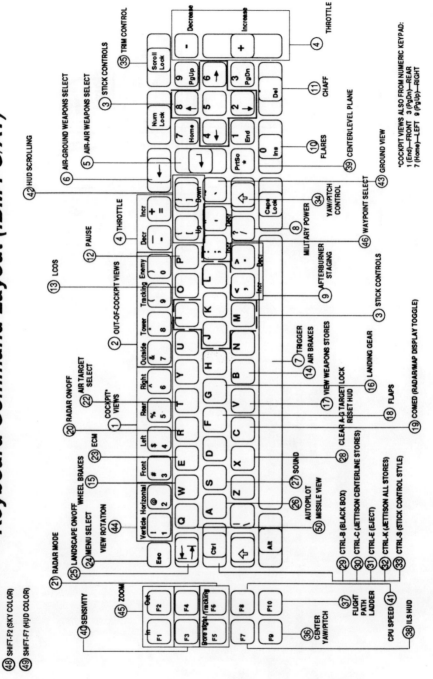

47 SHIFT-F1 (GROUND COLOR)
48 SHIFT-F2 (SKY COLOR)
49 SHIFT-F7 (HUD COLOR)

21 RADAR MODE
25 LANDSCAPE ON/OFF WHEEL BRAKES
24 MENU SELECT
44 VIEW ROTATION

20 RADAR ON/OFF
22 AIR TARGET SELECT
23 ECM
15 Front

42 HUD SCROLLING
35 TRIM CONTROL
3 STICK CONTROLS
6 AIR-GROUND WEAPONS SELECT
5 AIR-AIR WEAPONS SELECT

Decrease
Increase
4 THROTTLE
11 CHAFF
10 FLARES
43 CENTER/LEVEL PLANE
39 GROUND VIEW

*COCKPIT VIEWS ALSO FROM FROM NUMERIC PAD:
1 (End)—FRONT   3 (PgDn)—REAR
7 (Home)—LEFT   9 (PgUp)—RIGHT

13 LCOS
12 PAUSE
4 THROTTLE
2 OUT-OF-COCKPIT VIEWS
1 COCKPIT* VIEWS

Left Right Outside Tower Tracking Enemy
Rear
Vertical Horizontal

34 YAW/PITCH CONTROL
8 MILITARY POWER
9 AFTERBURNER STAGING
3 STICK CONTROLS
46 WAYPOINT SELECT

7 TRIGGER
14 AIR BRAKES
17 CLEAR A-G TARGET LOCK RESET HUD
16 LANDING GEAR
18 FLAPS
19 COMED (RADAR/MAP DISPLAY TOGGLE)

26 MISSILE VIEW
27 SOUND
28 CLEAR A-G (JETTISON CENTERLINE STORES)
50 AUTOPILOT

29 CTRL-B (BLACK BOX)
30 CTRL-C (JETTISON CENTERLINE STORES)
31 CTRL-E (EJECT)
32 CTRL-K (JETTISON ALL STORES)
33 CTRL-S (STICK CONTROL STYLE)

40 SENSIVITY
45 ZOOM
In Out
Bore sight/Tracking

37 FLIGHT PATH LADDER
36 CENTER YAW/PITCH
41 CPU SPEED
38 ILS HUD

Numeric Keypad

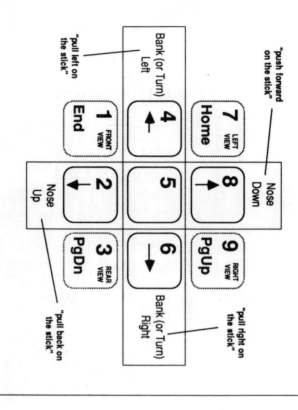

"push forward on the stick" — Nose Down

"pull right on the stick"

Bank (or Turn) Left — "pull left on the stick"

7 Home	8 Nose Down	9 PgUp RIGHT VIEW
4 ←	5	6 → Bank (or Turn) Right
1 End FRONT VIEW	2 ← Nose Up	3 PgDn REAR VIEW

"pull back on the stick"

IBM is a registered trademark and IBM PC is a trademark of International Business Machines Corporation.

Joystick

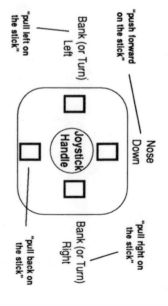

"push forward on the stick" — Nose Down

"pull right on the stick"

Bank (or Turn) Left — "pull left on the stick"

Joystick Handle

Bank (or Turn) Right

"pull back on the stick"

Joystick Button 1 - Trigger (used for firing weapons)

Joystick Button 2 - Weapons Select (alternative to toggling through HUD modes with **Enter** or **Backspace** key. After selecting either "Air-to-Air" or "Air-to-Ground" HUD mode with the forementioned keys, you can click Button 2 and toggle through the different weapons types possible in either A-A or A-G category. If you wish to change from A-A to A-G, or vice-versa, you'll still need to press either the **Enter** or **Backspace** key once (depending on the mode desired).

The FALCON AT™ Landscape Map

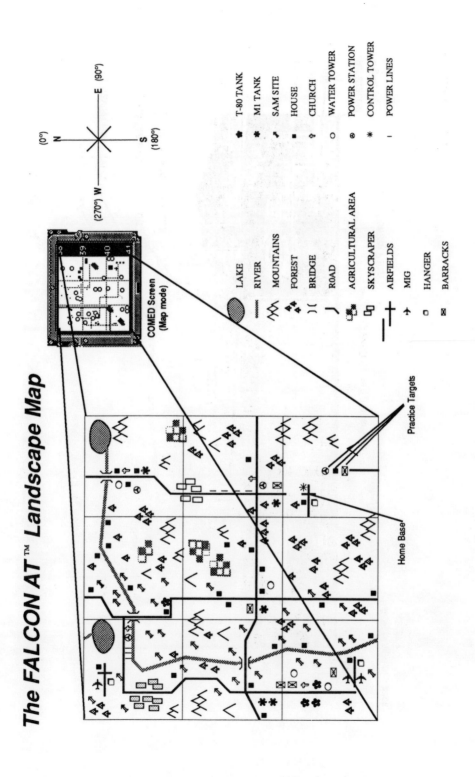

N (0°)

W (270°)   E (90°)

S (180°)

COMED Screen
(Map mode)

Practice Targets

Home Base

LAKE		T-80 TANK
RIVER		M1 TANK
MOUNTAINS		SAM SITE
FOREST		HOUSE
BRIDGE		CHURCH
ROAD		WATER TOWER
AGRICULTURAL AREA		POWER STATION
SKYSCRAPER		CONTROL TOWER
AIRFIELDS		POWER LINES
MIG		
HANGER		
BARRACKS		

The FALCON AT Cockpit (Main Features)

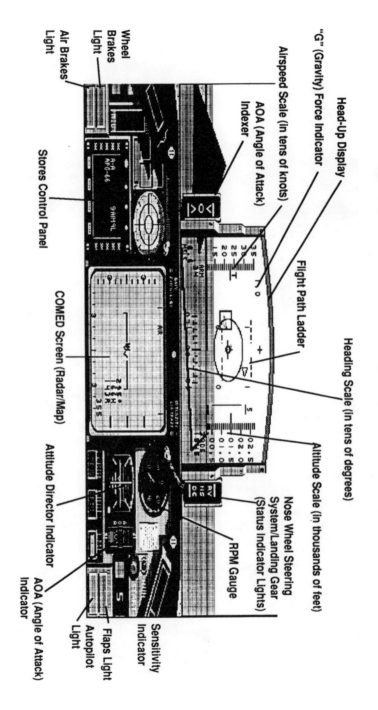

Head-Up Display

"G" (Gravity) Force Indicator

Airspeed Scale (in tens of knots)

AOA (Angle of Attack) Indexer

Wheel Brakes Light

Air Brakes Light

Stores Control Panel

COMED Screen (Radar/Map)

Attitude Director Indicator

AOA (Angle of Attack) Indicator

Autopilot Light

Flaps Light

Sensitivity Indicator

RPM Gauge

Nose Wheel Steering System/Landing Gear (Status Indicator Lights)

Altitude Scale (in thousands of feet)

Heading Scale (in tens of degrees)

Flight Path Ladder

FALCON™ Keyboard Command Layout (IBM ® PC™)

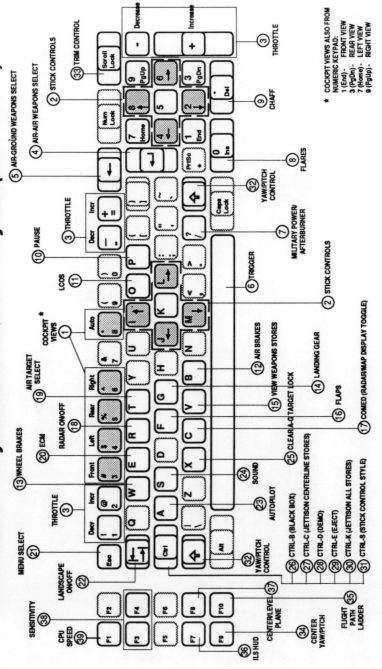

* COCKPIT VIEWS ALSO FROM
  NUMERIC KEYPAD:
  1 (End) - FRONT VIEW
  3 (PgDn) - REAR VIEW
  7 (Home) - LEFT VIEW
  9 (PgUp) - RIGHT VIEW

① COCKPIT VIEWS *
② STICK CONTROLS
③ THROTTLE
④ AIR-AIR WEAPONS SELECT
⑤ AIR-GROUND WEAPONS SELECT
⑥ TRIGGER
⑦ MILITARY POWER/AFTERBURNER
⑧ FLARES
⑨ CHAFF
⑩ PAUSE
⑪ LCOS
⑫ AIR BRAKES
⑬ WHEEL BRAKES
⑭ LANDING GEAR
⑮ VIEW WEAPONS STORES
⑯ FLAPS
⑰ COMED (RADAR/MAP DISPLAY TOGGLE)
⑱ RADAR ON/OFF
⑲ AIR TARGET SELECT
⑳ ECM
㉑ MENU SELECT
㉒ LANDSCAPE ON/OFF
㉓ AUTOPILOT
㉔ SOUND
㉕ CLEAR/A-G TARGET LOCK
㉖ CTRL-B (BLACK BOX)
㉗ CTRL-C (JETTISON CENTERLINE STORES)
㉘ CTRL-D (DEMO)
㉙ CTRL-E (EJECT)
㉚ CTRL-K (JETTISON ALL STORES)
㉛ CTRL-S (STICK CONTROL STYLE)
㉜ YAW/PITCH CONTROL
㉝ TRIM CONTROL
㉞ CENTER YAW/PITCH
㉟ FLIGHT PATH LADDER
㊱ ILS HUD
㊲ CENTER LEVEL PLANE
㊳ SENSITIVITY
㊴ CPU SPEED

Numeric Keypad

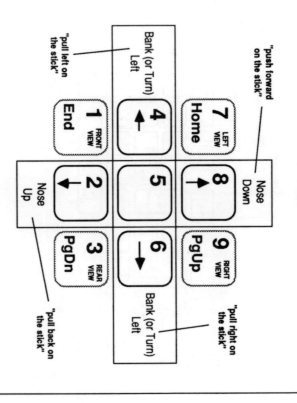

"push forward on the stick" — Nose Down

"pull left on the stick"

Bank (or Turn) Left

7 LEFT VIEW Home	8 ↑	9 RIGHT VIEW PgUp
4 ←	5	6 →
1 FRONT VIEW End	2 ←	3 REAR VIEW PgDn

Bank (or Turn) Left

"pull back on the stick" — Nose Up

"pull right on the stick"

Joystick

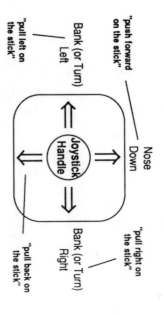

"push forward on the stick" — Nose Down

"pull left on the stick"

Bank (or Turn) Left

Joystick Handle

"pull right on the stick"

Bank (or Turn) Right

"pull back on the stick"

Joystick Button 1 - Trigger (used for firing weapons)

Joystick Button 2 - Weapons Select (alternative to toggling through HUD modes with **Enter** or **Backspace** key. After selecting either "Air-to-Air" or "Air-to-Ground" HUD mode with the forementioned keys, you can click Button 2 and toggle through the different weapons types possible in either A-A or A-G category. If you wish to change from A-A to A-G, or vice-versa, you'll still need to press either the **Enter** or **Backspace** key once (depending on the mode desired).

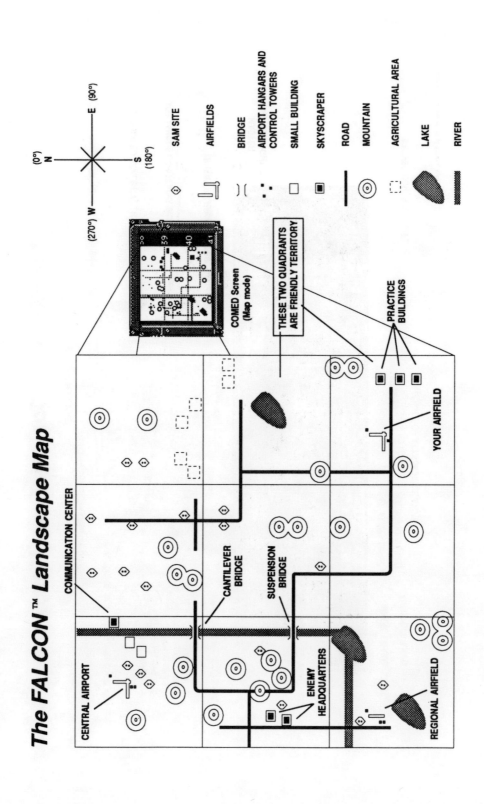

The FALCON™ Landscape Map

SAM SITE
AIRFIELDS
BRIDGE
AIRPORT HANGARS AND CONTROL TOWERS
SMALL BUILDING
SKYSCRAPER
ROAD
MOUNTAIN
AGRICULTURAL AREA
LAKE
RIVER

N (0°)
E (90°)
S (180°)
W (270°)

COMED Screen (Map mode)

THESE TWO QUADRANTS ARE FRIENDLY TERRITORY

PRACTICE BUILDINGS

COMMUNICATION CENTER

CENTRAL AIRPORT

CANTILEVER BRIDGE

SUSPENSION BRIDGE

ENEMY HEADQUARTERS

REGIONAL AIRFIELD

YOUR AIRFIELD

The FALCON™ Cockpit (Front View)

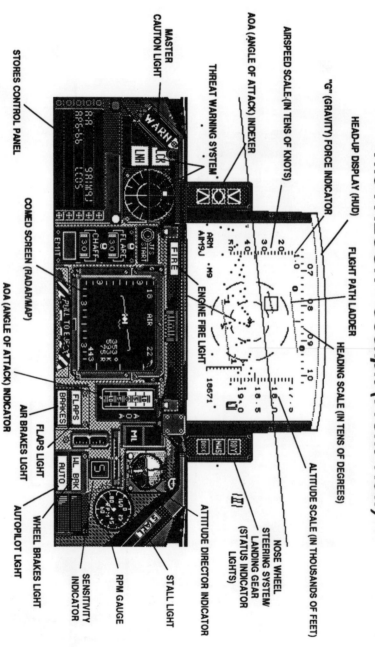

HEAD-UP DISPLAY (HUD)

"G" (GRAVITY) FORCE INDICATOR

AIRSPEED SCALE (IN TENS OF KNOTS)

AOA (ANGLE OF ATTACK) INDEXER

THREAT WARNING SYSTEM

MASTER CAUTION LIGHT

STORES CONTROL PANEL

COMED SCREEN (RADAR/MAP)

AOA (ANGLE OF ATTACK) INDICATOR

FLAPS LIGHT

AIR BRAKES LIGHT

AUTOPILOT LIGHT

WHEEL BRAKES LIGHT

SENSITIVITY INDICATOR

RPM GAUGE

STALL LIGHT

ATTITUDE DIRECTOR INDICATOR

NOSE WHEEL STEERING SYSTEM/ LANDING GEAR (STATUS INDICATOR LIGHTS)

ALTITUDE SCALE (IN THOUSANDS OF FEET)

HEADING SCALE (IN TENS OF DEGREES)

FLIGHT PATH LADDER

ENGINE FIRE LIGHT

FALCON™ Keyboard Commands (Standard Macintosh™ Keyboard)

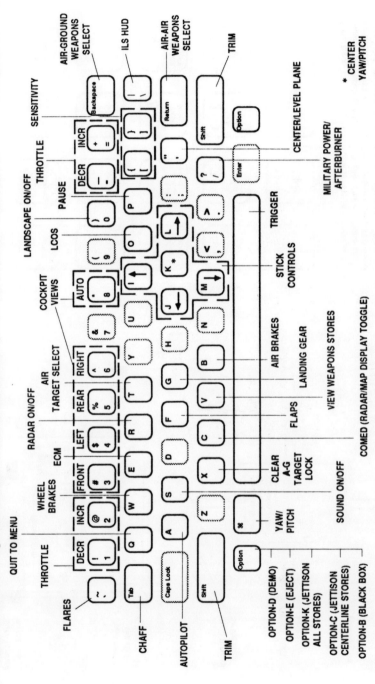

Note: If you have a Macintosh Plus keyboard or later model from Apple*, the amount and/or locations of the "\" (Backslash), Option, and "⌘" (Command) keys may differ from these descriptions. However, they are functionally identical.

Numeric Keypad

Clear CLEAR A-G TARGET LOCK	**=** A-A WEAPONS SELECT	**/** A-G WEAPONS SELECT	***** AFTER- BURNER
7 LEFT VIEW	**8** PUSH STICK FORWARD	**9** RIGHT VIEW	**-** DECREASE THROTTLE
4 PULL STICK LEFT	**5** CENTER YAW/ PITCH	**6** PULL STICK RIGHT	**+** INCREASE THROTTLE
1 FRONT VIEW	**2** PULL STICK BACK	**3** REAR VIEW	**Enter**
0 TRIGGER		**.** CHAFF	**FLARES**

Note: If you have the older style numeric keypad that was sold separately by Apple (model # M0120), the command "locations" are identical to the layout shown here, although some of the keys are labeled differently. For example, the "+" (plus) key shown here for Throttle Increase is the "," (comma) key instead on your pad. However, it performs the same function.

Kraft® QuickStick™

SET SWITCH TO "J" (FOR JOYSTICK)

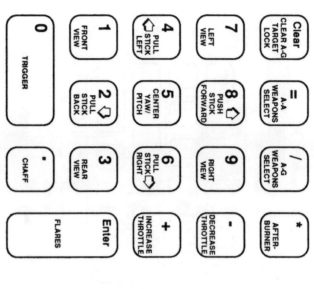

Mouse

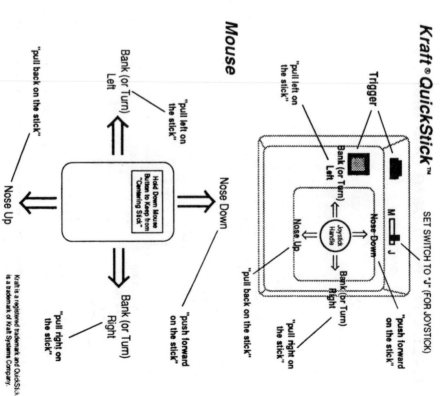

Hold Down Mouse Button to Keep from "Centering Stick"

Bank (or Turn) Left — "pull left on the stick"

Nose Down — "push forward on the stick"

Bank (or Turn) Right — "pull right on the stick"

Nose Up — "pull back on the stick"

Kraft is a registered trademark and QuickStick is a trademark of Kraft Systems Company.

The FALCON™ Landscape Map

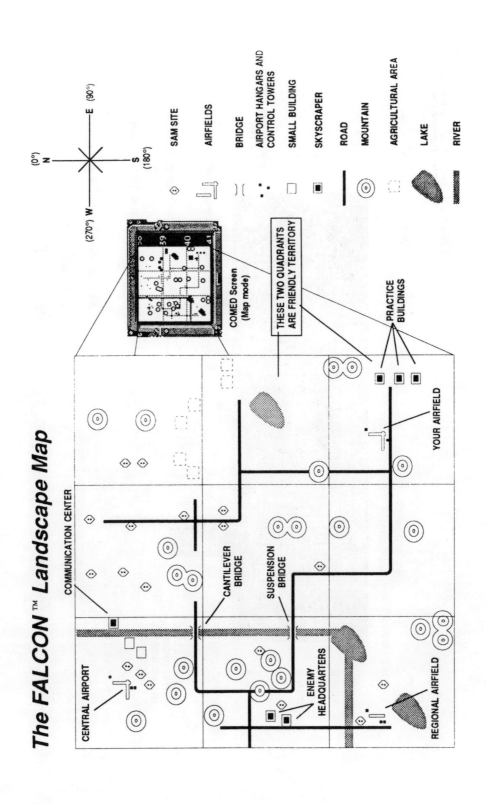

N (0°)

W (270°)   E (90°)

S (180°)

SAM SITE

AIRFIELDS

BRIDGE

AIRPORT HANGARS AND
CONTROL TOWERS

SMALL BUILDING

SKYSCRAPER

ROAD

MOUNTAIN

AGRICULTURAL AREA

LAKE

RIVER

COMED Screen
(Map mode)

THESE TWO QUADRANTS
ARE FRIENDLY TERRITORY

PRACTICE
BUILDINGS

YOUR AIRFIELD

COMMUNICATION CENTER

CENTRAL AIRPORT

CANTILEVER
BRIDGE

SUSPENSION
BRIDGE

ENEMY
HEADQUARTERS

REGIONAL AIRFIELD

The FALCON™ Cockpit (Front View)

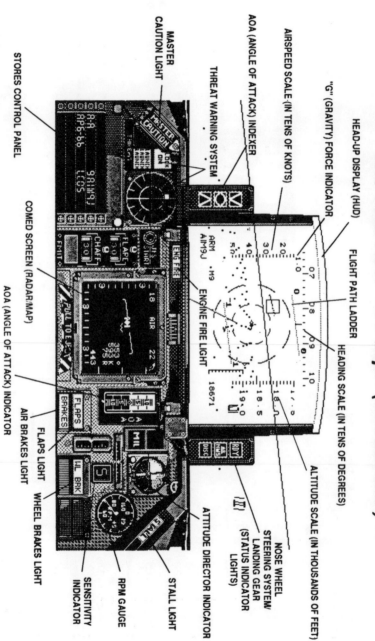

HEAD-UP DISPLAY (HUD)

"G" (GRAVITY) FORCE INDICATOR

AIRSPEED SCALE (IN TENS OF KNOTS)

AOA (ANGLE OF ATTACK) INDEXER

THREAT WARNING SYSTEM

MASTER CAUTION LIGHT

STORES CONTROL PANEL

COMED SCREEN (RADAR/MAP)

AOA (ANGLE OF ATTACK) INDICATOR

FLAPS LIGHT

AIR BRAKES LIGHT

WHEEL BRAKES LIGHT

SENSITIVITY INDICATOR

RPM GAUGE

STALL LIGHT

ATTITUDE DIRECTOR INDICATOR

ENGINE FIRE LIGHT

FLIGHT PATH LADDER

HEADING SCALE (IN TENS OF DEGREES)

ALTITUDE SCALE (IN THOUSANDS OF FEET)

NOSE WHEEL STEERING SYSTEM/ LANDING GEAR (STATUS INDICATOR LIGHTS)

KEYBOARD COMMAND LAYOUT FOR ATARI ST AND AMIGA

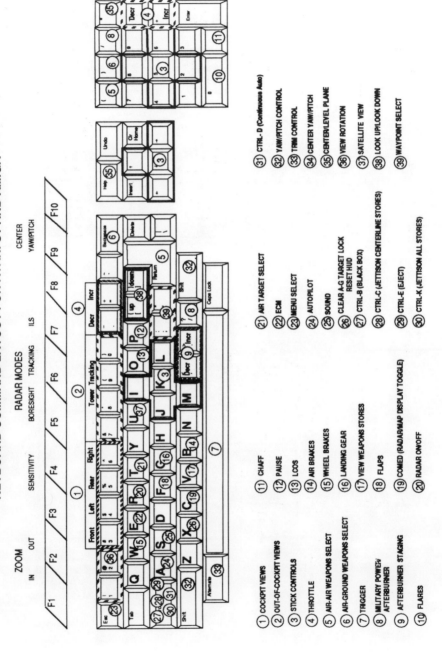

① COCKPIT VIEWS
② OUT-OF-COCKPIT VIEWS
③ STICK CONTROLS
④ THROTTLE
⑤ AIR-AIR WEAPONS SELECT
⑥ AIR-GROUND WEAPONS SELECT
⑦ TRIGGER
⑧ MILITARY POWER/ AFTERBURNER
⑨ AFTERBURNER STAGING
⑩ FLARES

⑪ CHAFF
⑫ PAUSE
⑬ LOCS
⑭ AIR BRAKES
⑮ WHEEL BRAKES
⑯ LANDING GEAR
⑰ VIEW WEAPONS STORES
⑱ FLAPS
⑲ COMED (RADAR/MAP DISPLAY TOGGLE)
⑳ RADAR ON/OFF

㉑ AIR TARGET SELECT
㉒ ECM
㉓ MENU SELECT
㉔ AUTOPILOT
㉕ SOUND
㉖ CLEAR A-G TARGET LOCK RESET HUD
㉗ CTRL-B (BLACK BOX)
㉘ CTRL-C (JETTISON CENTERLINE STORES)
㉙ CTRL-E (EJECT)
㉚ CTRL-X (JETTISON ALL STORES)

㉛ CTRL- D (Continuous Auto)
㉜ YAW/PITCH CONTROL
㉝ TRIM CONTROL
㉞ CENTER YAW/PITCH
㉟ CENTER/LEVEL PLANE
㊱ VIEW ROTATION
㊲ SATELLITE VIEW
㊳ LOOK UP/LOOK DOWN
㊴ WAYPOINT SELECT

Numeric Keypad

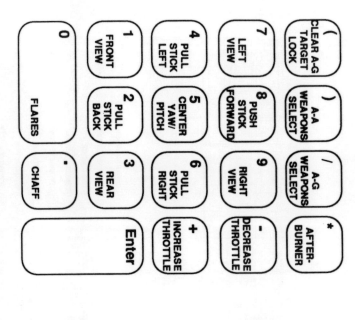

Form FALAST70

Keypad keys:
- (CLEAR A-G TARGET LOCK
-) A-A WEAPONS SELECT
- / A-G WEAPONS SELECT
- * AFTER-BURNER
- 7 LEFT VIEW
- 8 PUSH STICK FORWARD
- 9 RIGHT VIEW
- - DECREASE THROTTLE
- 4 PULL STICK LEFT
- 5 CENTER YAW/ PITCH
- 6 PULL STICK RIGHT
- + INCREASE THROTTLE
- 1 FRONT VIEW
- 2 PULL STICK BACK
- 3 REAR VIEW
- Enter
- 0 FLARES
- . CHAFF

Joystick

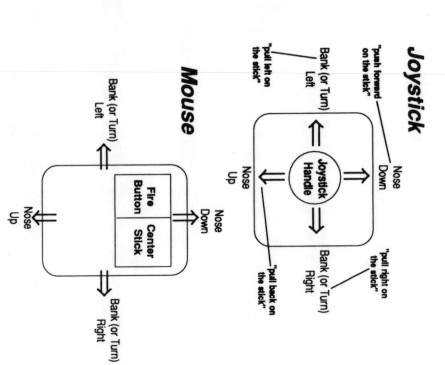

"push forward on the stick"

Nose Down

Bank (or Turn) Left

"pull left on the stick"

Joystick Handle

Nose Up

Bank (or Turn) Right

"pull right on the stick"

"pull back on the stick"

Mouse

Bank (or Turn) Left

Fire Button

Center Stick

Nose Down

Nose Up

Bank (or Turn) Right

The FALCON™ Landscape Map

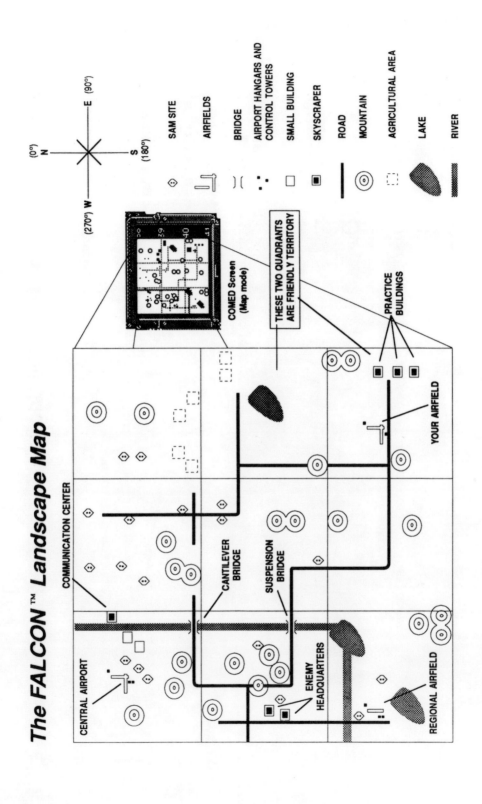

N (0°)
W (270°)   E (90°)
S (180°)

SAM SITE

AIRFIELDS

BRIDGE

AIRPORT HANGARS AND
CONTROL TOWERS

SMALL BUILDING

SKYSCRAPER

ROAD

MOUNTAIN

AGRICULTURAL AREA

LAKE

RIVER

COMED Screen
(Map mode)

THESE TWO QUADRANTS
ARE FRIENDLY TERRITORY

PRACTICE
BUILDINGS

YOUR AIRFIELD

COMMUNICATION CENTER

CENTRAL AIRPORT

CANTILEVER
BRIDGE

SUSPENSION
BRIDGE

ENEMY
HEADQUARTERS

REGIONAL AIRFIELD

The FALCON Cockpit (Front View)

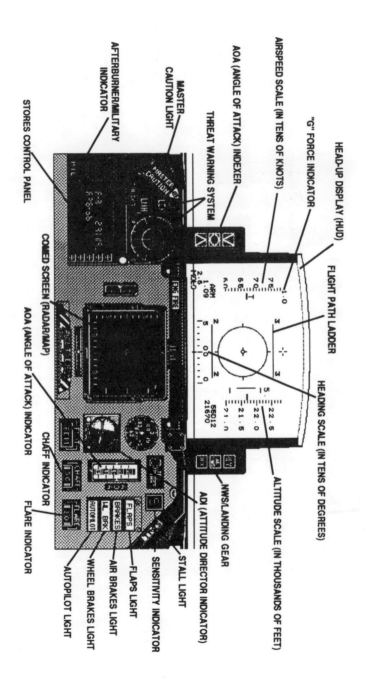

- HEAD-UP DISPLAY (HUD)
- "G" FORCE INDICATOR
- AIRSPEED SCALE (IN TENS OF KNOTS)
- AOA (ANGLE OF ATTACK) INDEXER
- THREAT WARNING SYSTEM
- MASTER CAUTION LIGHT
- AFTERBURNER/MILITARY INDICATOR
- STORES CONTROL PANEL
- COMED SCREEN (RADAR/MAP)
- AOA (ANGLE OF ATTACK) INDICATOR
- CHAFF INDICATOR
- FLARE INDICATOR
- AUTOPILOT LIGHT
- WHEEL BRAKES LIGHT
- AIR BRAKES LIGHT
- FLAPS LIGHT
- SENSITIVITY INDICATOR
- STALL LIGHT
- ADI (ATTITUDE DIRECTOR INDICATOR)
- NWS/LANDING GEAR
- ALTITUDE SCALE (IN THOUSANDS OF FEET)
- HEADING SCALE (IN TENS OF DEGREES)
- FLIGHT PATH LADDER

The FALCON™ Landscape Map

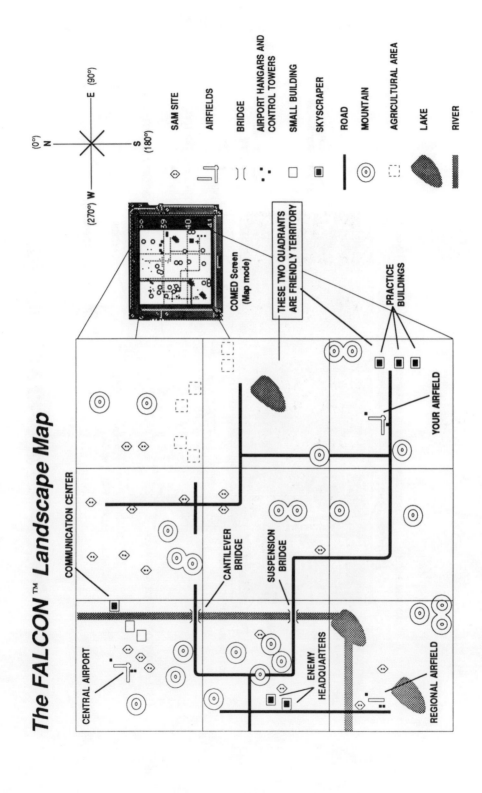

N (0°)
E (90°)
S (180°)
W (270°)

SAM SITE
AIRFIELDS
BRIDGE
AIRPORT HANGARS AND CONTROL TOWERS
SMALL BUILDING
SKYSCRAPER
ROAD
MOUNTAIN
AGRICULTURAL AREA
LAKE
RIVER

COMED Screen (Map mode)

THESE TWO QUADRANTS ARE FRIENDLY TERRITORY

PRACTICE BUILDINGS

YOUR AIRFIELD

COMMUNICATION CENTER

CENTRAL AIRPORT

CANTILEVER BRIDGE

SUSPENSION BRIDGE

ENEMY HEADQUARTERS

REGIONAL AIRFIELD

The FALCON Cockpit (Front View)

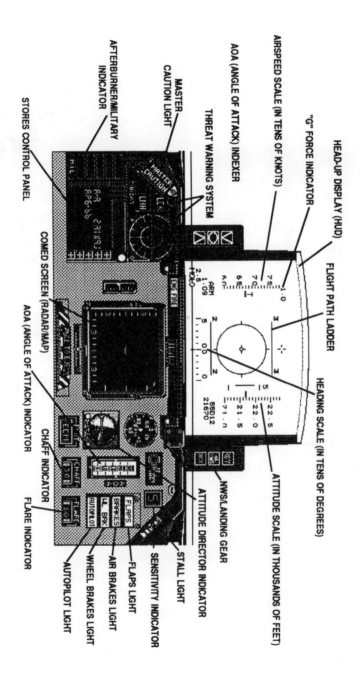

AFTERBURNER/MILITARY INDICATOR

MASTER CAUTION LIGHT

STORES CONTROL PANEL

THREAT WARNING SYSTEM

AOA (ANGLE OF ATTACK) INDEXER

AIRSPEED SCALE (IN TENS OF KNOTS)

"G" FORCE INDICATOR

HEAD-UP DISPLAY (HUD)

FLIGHT PATH LADDER

HEADING SCALE (IN TENS OF DEGREES)

ATTITUDE SCALE (IN THOUSANDS OF FEET)

NWS/LANDING GEAR

ATTITUDE DIRECTOR INDICATOR

STALL LIGHT

SENSITIVITY INDICATOR

FLAPS LIGHT

AIR BRAKES LIGHT

WHEEL BRAKES LIGHT

AUTOPILOT LIGHT

FLARE INDICATOR

CHAFF INDICATOR

AOA (ANGLE OF ATTACK) INDICATOR

COMED SCREEN (RADAR/MAP)

Other Great Simulations from
Spectrum HoloByte™

Falcon Missions Disk: The Falcon Missions Disk offers completely new missions which add dramatically to the original game. The scenario is now filled with new targets, new landscape, extra strategy elements, and more and deadlier enemies. Atari ST, Amiga: $24.95

PT-109: Climb aboard the PT-109 patrol boat and control your vessel around islands where other ships are unable to go. The enemy is present in the air as well as the sea, so make the most effective use of your arsenal of weapons such as torpedoes, depth charges, and rockets.
Mac: $49.95, IBM: $39.95

Tank: Our latest project, Tank simulates the US Army's number one ground weapon, the M1-A1 Abrams battlefield tank. You will maneuver this seemingly indestructable machine over rough terrain while using dangerous weapons at your discretion. IBM: $59.95

Vette!: This red hot new street racing simulation sends you racing other classic sports cars through the hilly streets of San Francisco. The game features accurate mapping of the city, multiple-view perspectives, 3-D solid modeling graphics and real maneuverability. IBM: $49.95

Orders Only: 1-800-729-4050
Spectrum HoloByte™
2061 Challenger Drive, Alameda, CA 94501